THE QUAKERS AS PIONEERS IN
SOCIAL WORK

THE
QUAKERS AS PIONEERS
IN SOCIAL WORK

(Studien über die Sozialpolitik der Quäker)

By

AUGUSTE JORNS, Dr. Rer. Pol.

Translated by

THOMAS KITE BROWN, Jr., Ph.D.

KENNIKAT PRESS, INC./PORT WASHINGTON, N. Y.

THE QUAKERS AS PIONEERS IN SOCIAL WORK

First published 1931
Reissued 1969 by Kennikat Press

Library of Congress Catalog Card No: 68-8232
Manufactured in the United States of America

AUTHOR'S PREFACE

THE material which constitutes the basis of the following investigation was collected for the most part in the Friends' Reference Library, Devonshire House, London E. C., where I was very kindly granted admission and access to all the old manuscripts, and where a great deal of courteous assistance was extended to me in the course of my researches. To the Society of Friends, and especially to the librarian, Dr. Norman Penney, F.S.A., who was of continuous assistance during the preparation of the manuscript, and who kindly read the proofs of the present edition in English, I acknowledge my cordial thanks.

I hope that I shall occasion no offense among those who call themselves "Friends" by using the designation "Quaker." It was only the fact that the official name is relatively unknown in Germany that determined me to adopt this course.

I should like also to use this occasion to draw attention to the fact that my work is independent of a book by D. von Dobbeler, which discusses the same subject, entitled *Sozialpolitik der Nächstenliebe* (Christian charity as a sociological theory), which appeared in the spring of the year 1912, whereas my manuscript was completed in December, 1911.

BIBLIOGRAPHICAL NOTE

Among the sources that were used in the preparation of this work was the following manuscript material, available at the Friends' Reference Library, Devonshire House, London E. C. (since removed to Friends House, Euston Road, London N. W. 1):

Minute Books of the Yearly Meeting (London), 1681-1857.
Minute Books of the Meeting for Sufferings.
Minute Books of Longford, Southwark, and Peel Monthly Meetings, 1705-1715, and a few from earlier and later years.
Trust Property Books of twelve quarterly meetings.
Register Books.
Sundry Ancient Epistles, a bound collection of manuscript material.
Manuscript of Fox's Journal.

Throughout the book, the following references, recurring rather frequently, are used to indicate the books named:

Beck and Ball: William Beck and T. Frederick Ball, *The London Friends' Meetings, Showing the Rise of the Society of Friends in London, with Accounts of the Various Meeting Houses and Burial Grounds,* London 1869.

Besse's *Sufferings:* Joseph Besse, *A Collection of the Sufferings of the People Called Quakers . . . Taken from Original Records and Other Authentic Accounts,* 1753.

Discipline: Book of Christian Discipline of the Religious Society of Friends, London 1883.

Journal: The Journal of George Fox, being an Historical Account of his Life, Travels, Sufferings, and Christian Experiences, in two volumes, London 1901.

Yearly Meeting Epistles: Epistles from the Yearly Meeting of Friends Held in London, two volumes, London 1858.

FOREWORD

In a period like the present, when the upheaval of modern civilization following the Great War has led to the most vital changes in every field of social and industrial life, the publication of a book written twenty years ago would seem to require a word of explanation. This may be found in the fact that it is the study of a small cross section of the great body of people calling themselves Christians, as to their conduct and relation to their fellow men in certain definite aspects of life. Since history, for centuries, has been repeating itself, it has seemed profitable to the sponsors of this translation to welcome a view of the Quaker from the standpoint of an outsider, who has, however, sympathetically presented the Quaker's early efforts to follow the injunctions of his divine Master.

The present time has brought forth, especially in England, a large number of individual studies of Quakers and of Quaker business firms.[1] There is, however, a dearth of writers who have studied the practical application of the Quaker theory to actual economic conditions. This is especially needed at the present day. With Quakerism, particularly in its middle period, corporate action

[1] For instance, Isabel Grubb has given us a valuable review of conditions in Great Britain, in *Quakers in Industry before 1800*. See also R. H. Tawney, *Religion and the Rise of Capitalism,* London 1929; Philip S. Belasco, *Authority in Church and State,* London 1928.

for many years was timid, while from the very start the individual Quaker has been bold as a lion. Quakerism has never dissociated industrial, economic or social life from the spiritual or religious sphere of action. It agrees in this respect with a far distant past, when, in the centuries before Luther, the Church held sway over all the daily activities and human interests of its members. Quakerism is, indeed, a "conduct of life," and when the modern world, in the agonies of struggle and pain, sought for a neutral people to come to its aid, Quakerism possessed the experience and the ability at once to answer the call.

Little did the author of this book dream of the chasm so soon to open between her and the nation where she had quietly pursued her task. A translation was proposed in this country immediately after its publication in German in 1912, but the outbreak of the war made the work at that time impossible. In the interval of nearly two decades which has passed, Quakerism has had to cast off some of its earlier forms, and readjust itself to new tasks and conditions. But the present can never be properly understood without a knowledge of the past, and it is profitable for students of our modern complicated industrial problems to follow the author's studies and endeavor to understand the motives of those "Children of the Light" who, in the seventeenth century, revived the relation between conscience and commerce which had largely been lost by their contemporaries.

The first half century of Quaker persecution was followed by the prosperity which always accompanies thrift and strict honesty; and his exclusion from the universities, because of his nonconformity, placed the Quaker in a position where he was willing to bear the cross of being unlike his fellows—of being "different." In this he shared the extreme individualism of the Puritan age and that immediately subsequent to it. The Methodist had somewhat the same experience. Both became rich; and John Wesley is quoted as saying that no religious revival could last long, because the virtues of industry, honesty and self-control which it engenders cause a poor man to become rich, and wealth is always the snare of the prosperous.

The Quaker had to bear some of the slanders of the time, because of his caution. "Sly" was a favorite epithet for him in the popular plays of his early day. But this he lived down, and Dr. Jorns has shown how, in the relief of the poor and the insane, in education, in prison reform, in the battle against alcoholism, in justice in trade and commerce, and the origin of the one-price idea, and especially in the antislavery movement, the Quaker has been in the van of economic and philanthropic endeavor. The world expects more of those whose profession is high, and Quakerism sets a high standard. The meetings closely followed the conduct of individual members, and one who erred in the Quaker garb brought reproach upon the entire body. Since Friends refused all aid from or communication with the parish, they must needs establish a system of their own, which they did at once. The Meeting for Sufferings at London, still functioning under its picturesque name, although with widely diversified interests, was established in 1676 to provide care and relief for the imprisoned Quakers suffering in England's loathsome dungeons. The strength of their form of organization is largely due to the natural development of its various parts as the need arose. They paid at the start a heavy price, not for their evil deeds, but for the simple fact that they were Quakers. We are told that in 1683 one hundred and seventy-eight Quakers in Bristol alone were imprisoned or fined, the prison sentences ranging from three to eleven months, and the fines totaling sixteen thousand pounds—an enormous sum for those days. But the price for freedom of life and thought was paid willingly.

Attention should be called to the fact that since the publication of this book, the complete Journal of George Fox, edited from the original manuscript by Dr. Norman Penney, has appeared, with notes which would have greatly aided the author. She had however access to the original manuscripts themselves. The London *Discipline* quoted has been superseded by the later *Christian Life, Faith, and Thought* of 1922. There are many helpful volumes which have come out since the war, greatly stimulating study in the field of economics and philanthropy. But the reader will find that these early efforts point helpfully toward the course necessarily to be followed by the Quaker of the twentieth century.

The seventeenth-century work of John Bellers was of the first importance in pointing out possible lines of reform in the industrial and philanthropic fields. The soundness of his principles was amply corroborated by Sir Frederick Eden a century later, and by Eden's contemporaries, the Quaker physicians and philanthropists, Fothergill and Lettsom. We have to-day several advanced Quaker employers in England and in the Middle States of America, who are their direct successors. There are still many thousand slaves in the world, despite the labors of John Woolman and his Quaker followers, and prisons with crowded inmates are still loudly calling for reform. Preventive measures were the great contribution inaugurated by Quakerism, as here studied, and this is the only course to be sought to-day. The Quaker idea is fundamental. A vast deal more of mental effort must be put forth to comprehend the situation, and then to apply the cure. Only a constructive Quakerism can reach and remedy the situation, and having started in the van, it should make every effort to keep its position. Social legislation must be attained to accomplish the great ends desired. The Quakers in the Pennsylvania Assembly of 1756 removed themselves in a body from a political crisis. Better counsels should now prevail, and the Quaker of to-day in the United States must not shrink from reëntrance into the political arena; for individual effort, however laudable and successful, must become national, and this can only be done through the body politic. Quaker statesmanship must be created and must come to the fore, fearless and enlightened, able to ignore the buffets from outside and the timidity within, for the Quaker as a social prophet has a challenge in present conditions, and an unprecedented opportunity.

AMELIA MOTT GUMMERE

CONTENTS

THE QUAKERS AS PIONEERS IN
SOCIAL WORK

INTRODUCTION

BRIEF OUTLINE OF THE QUAKER MOVEMENT

THE Quakers constitute one of those numerous religious groups which arose in England in the seventeenth
century.[1] It was the period in which, with the weakening
of the power of the crown, the popular opposition to the
officially recognized Reformation developed so power-
fully that church and state were shaken to their foundations. Puritanism, as this whole movement is called,
arose as early as the reign of Bloody Mary. In 1554
occurred the first schism among the English Protestants,
in the community of fugitives in Frankfort, and after
their return to England [2] the revolt against Episcopal
domination began, first within and then outside the Estab-

[1] For the history of the Quaker movement the best of earlier works is
William Sewel, *The History of the Rise, Increase, and Progress of the
Christian People Called Quakers,* London 1722 (originally issued in Low
Dutch in 1717). The standard works now are William C. Braithwaite,
The Beginnings of Quakerism, London 1912, and *The Second Period of
Quakerism,* London 1919; Rufus M. Jones, *The Later Periods of Quaker-
ism,* 2 vols., London 1921. Of smaller works, T. Edmund Harvey, *The
Rise of the Quakers* (vol. v of *Eras of Nonconformity*), London 1905,
and Elizabeth Braithwaite Emmott's two books *The Story of Quakerism,*
London 1908 (new edition, enlarged, London 1929), and *A Short History
of Quakerism,* London 1923, are to be recommended. Various histories of
Quakerism in specific countries have been written, of which Allen C.
Thomas and Richard H. Thomas, *A History of the Friends in America*
(1st edition 1894), 6th edition, revised, Philadelphia 1930, and Rufus M.
Jones (assisted by Isaac Sharpless and Amelia M. Gummere), *The
Quakers in the American Colonies,* London 1911, may be mentioned.
[2] After the beginning of Elizabeth's reign, in 1558.

lished Church. All attempts at effecting any radical
change, however, were held in check as long as burning at
the stake threatened those who wished to commune with
their God in any other way than through the legally prescribed forms. Many Protestants succeeded, in spite of
laws which prohibited emigration, in escaping persecution
by flight; they found a hospitable reception in Holland
and Germany, and were influenced in many ways by the
different trends of the Reformation on the Continent.
Under the first Stuarts a few of them ventured back to
England, and there strengthened the attack on the Established Church (which was disestablished in 1643), but at
the same time they increased the tendency toward fac-
tionalism among the opponents of the Church. An absolutely incomprehensible number of parties arose, each one
fighting for its own ideal form of church; there was
hardly any imaginable type of creed or of Divine service
which did not have its supporters.[3]

One group of Puritans, of considerable strength, maintained the Scotch Presbyterian creed; and three years
after the disestablishment of the Episcopal Church, this
creed had risen to the point of being officially adopted,
even though it lacked from the very first the elements of
permanence. As Neal[4] points out, it was a fatal mistake

[3] S. R. Gardiner, *Fall of the Monarchy of Charles I*, London 1882,
ii, 247. "For the mass of Englishmen, religious belief was their only
intellectual food, as religious books were their only literature. There
were thousands for whom legal and constitutional arguments had but
little attraction, who could throw their whole souls into an argument
about Presbyterianism or Episcopacy, or about the comparative merits of
various forms of worship."

[4] Daniel Neal, *History of the Puritans, or Protestant Nonconformists,
from the Reformation in 1517 to the Revolution in 1688,* revised edition
London 1837, ii, 271.

of Parliament to abolish one form of religious institution before agreeing upon another to take its place; for in the interregnum the dissenters could increase so much that no uniformity or agreement could ever again be attained. The intolerance of the Presbyterians hastened their fall; as early as 1649 an uprising brought to the helm the so-called Independents, one group of which had taken refuge in Middelburg, Zealand, led by the Englishman Robert Browne, with principles involving a greater degree of liberty than had ever before been dreamed of. Though this movement comprised, in its earlier days, prominent and highly educated men,[5] during the stress of the Civil Wars it expanded so as to include the masses of the people, and tended toward prophesying and religious ecstasy. From the Independents arose the Saints. But these latter strove earnestly for peace; and it is thus only a natural consequence that the period of their dominance saw the first religious liberty [6] granted to Episcopalians as well as to the various sects which cultivated the religious ecstasy and kindred experiences. Quakerism, too, found opportunity to develop under these auspices.

The history of its origin and first expansion is at the same time the history of its founder, George Fox.[7] This

[5] For example, Henry Barrowe, John Greenwood, Francis Johnson, Henry Ainsworth, John Robinson (leader of the Pilgrim Fathers), and even Milton and Cromwell.

[6] Placed under official regulation September 27, 1650, at which time the Acts of Uniformity of Elizabeth were repealed. See S. R. Gardiner, *Constitutional Documents of the Puritan Revolution,* 3d edition Oxford 1906, p. 391.

[7] The principal source of Fox's life is his Journal, probably compiled toward the end of his life from notes made earlier, with many letters by Fox. The manuscript, and the edition of 1891 (reprinted in 1901), have been used; references are to the edition of 1901: *The Journal of George*

remarkable man, whom Weingarten [8] calls the last English reformer, was born in Drayton, Leicestershire, in 1624 (exactly 300 years after the first reformer Wycliffe), the son of a weaver in modest circumstances. As his father had intended him to learn a trade, his instruction was limited to the elementary subjects; in accordance with the spirit of the times, instruction in religious matters formed the chief factor of his education. Fox's parents had a serious, puritanical attitude, though they did not separate from the Established Church; but to young George they had no consolation to offer—even in his early youth he was harassed by religious doubts. These doubts caused him, when he was only nineteen years old, to leave his master, a shoemaker [9] in Nottingham, and go to his uncle in London, who belonged to the Baptists.

But he did not stay long here either. Repelled by the

Fox, being an Historical account of his Life, Travels, Sufferings and Christian Experiences, in two volumes (hereafter referred to as Journal). Issued by the Society of Friends. London, Headley Brothers, 1901. Extracts from this work appeared in a German translation by Margarethe Stähelin under the title George Fox, Aufzeichnungen und Briefe des ersten Quäkers (Sketches and letters of the first Quaker), Tübingen, J. C. B. Mohr, 1908. The Cambridge University Press put out the text of the original manuscript in 1911: The Journal of George Fox, edited from the MSS by Norman Penney, F.S.A., usually called the Cambridge Journal; and also The Short Journal and Itinerary Journals of George Fox, Cambridge 1925, with the same editor. See also Thomas Hodgkin, George Fox, Boston and London 1896; A. Neave Brayshaw, The Personality of George Fox, London 1919; Rufus M. Jones, George Fox, Seeker and Friend, London and New York 1930.

[8] Hermann Weingarten, Die Revolutionskirchen Englands. Ein Beitrag zur internen Geschichte der englischen Kirche und der Reformation, Leipzig 1868.

[9] This master engaged also in cattle raising and selling wool; probably the tradition that Fox was a shepherd arises from this fact. Some records suggest that the apprenticeship was in Mancetter or Manchester. See Braithwaite, The Beginnings of Quakerism, p. 30; and Jones, George Fox, Seeker and Friend, pp. 13, 40ff.

godless life of many who called themselves Christians, he
sought in vain for counsel and help from clergymen of
various kinds, and finally withdrew from contact with any
of them, and began a life of restless wandering.[10] His
attitude of mind was as varied as his external history
during these years. Following upon a time of deepest
depression of soul there came a condition of being filled
with heavenly joy; and then again the yearning for truth
and spiritual perfection obliterated all other emotion. A
statement made by Rowntree [11] of many of the opponents
of the Established Church applies especially to him:
"Men were yearning to feel Christ closer to their spirits
. . . to know His gospel a real glad tidings to all, especially to those who lived in cottages and passed their days
in toil. Men had grown weary of disputings about
methods of Church government, whether by Popes, Bishops, Presbyters, or Ruling Elders. . . . Thus there was
a widespread yearning for a presentation of Christianity,
more spiritual and less theological, more ethical and less
dogmatic, more practical and less ceremonial, than that
then dominant."

Barclay [12] thinks it probable that there was hardly a
single religious movement with which Fox had not become
familiar during his wanderings. He may have uncon-

[10] *Journal*, i, 10: "I kept myself much as a stranger, seeking heavenly
wisdom and getting knowledge from the Lord; and was brought off
from outward things to rely wholly on the Lord alone."

[11] John S. Rowntree, *The Society of Friends, its Faith and Practice*,
3d edition London 1902, pp. 17, 18.

[12] Robert Barclay, *The Inner Life of the Religious Societies of the
Commonwealth*, 2d edition London 1877, p. 254. On the relation of
George Fox to the Mystics and to prophesying see also Theodor Sippel,
Über den Ursprung des Quäkertums (On the origin of Quakerism), in
Die Christliche Welt (The Christian world), 1910, Nos. 19-21.

sciously absorbed much of this experience into his inner
life, even though, according to his own view, he attained
inner clarity only through Divine revelation and intensive
study of the Bible. After long wandering about in lone-
liness, and wrestling in vain for light, just as all hope of
finding anybody to whom he could unburden his soul
seemed gone, he suddenly heard a voice which directed
him to Christ as the only Comforter and Adviser.[13] He
immediately felt that a great change had taken place in
him: God had given him renewed hope, but at the same
time had laid a sacred duty upon him, for he had shown
him, along with the vision of eternal glory, the dire sinfulness of mankind, and had put words into his mouth to
lead the church back to the long-forgotten Truth.

We cannot make it our task here to follow in detail the
doctrines of Quakerism in their gradual development, but
only to bring out their chief characteristics. At the central point of the whole is the doctrine of the Inner Light,
which illumines every man that comes into the world.
Whoever follows this Light will be freed of all evil. The
definition of this divinely animating principle in man is
not always the same; it is sometimes regarded as something distinct from the conscience, and sometimes identi-
fied with the conscience and at the same time with Christ
(*Christus mysticus,* William Penn). This uncertainty
might have been expected to give rise to speculations as to
the historical reality of the life of Jesus in Palestine;[14]

[13] *Journal,* i, 11.
[14] In this connection see also C. B. Hylkema, *Reformateurs. Geschied-
kundige Studien ever de Godsdienstige Bewegingen mit de Nadagan
onzer Gouden Euw* (Reformers. Historical studies of the religious movements to the end of the Golden Age), 2 vols., Haarlem 1900, ii, 357.

but the Quakers resolutely avoided the dangers of such speculation. Theological investigations also languish among them, because, according to their view, only personal experience can lead to an understanding of the true nature and significance of inspiration. Let each one work out his own salvation. The Divine power will support him; but let him not depend upon other men.

From the denial of the need of anyone to serve as mediator in attaining salvation, arising from their faith in the Inner Light, there resulted on the one hand their rejection of the clergy as a group set apart from the rest of the world, and on the other their insistence upon the universal priesthood of believers. This latter doctrine was also maintained by Independents, Separatists, Erastians,[15] and other sects, but was not carried through by them to its logical results. Whoever has attained to faith has the duty of showing others the way; but no one should seek his own advantage in activity of this sort.[16] God calls his helpers from all classes, women as well as men;[17] there is no need, according to the Quakers, of special preparation for the office of preaching, but on the contrary special study might destroy the working of the Holy

[15] See Neal, *op. cit.* ii, 264ff.
[16] William Penn, *Some Fruits of Solitude in Reflections and Maxims,* (first printed London 1693; quotations are from the edition by John Clifford, London 1905), p. 95 (part 1, §§ 462, 463): "As they freely receive from Christ, so they give. They will not make that a Trade, which they know ought not, in Conscience, to be one."
[17] The calling of women is based upon such passages in the Bible as 1 Cor. 11:4, 5: "Every man praying or prophesying, having his head covered, dishonoureth his head; but every woman that prayeth or prophesieth with her head uncovered dishonoureth her head: for that is even all one as if she were shaven." Passages in opposition to this point of view are explained as arising from special conditions of time or place, having only a temporary application.

25

Spirit in the human heart. Nor does Divine service, as
Christ himself instituted it, need any special external
forms.[18] The congregation therefore unites in quiet worship, which is supposed to open the heart to the Divine
Inner Light; and if anybody feels that a message is given
to him, he arises, and the Spirit of God speaks through
him to the assembly. This practice is liable to the danger
of degenerating into extravagant or fanatical ecstasies;
yet precautions are taken as far as possible to prevent this.
All those present in the congregation bear the responsibility for the character of the messages. The Book of
Discipline [19] reads: "Advised, that Ministers, as well as
Elders and others, in all their preaching, writing, and
conversing about the things of God, do keep to the form
of sound words or Scripture terms; and that none pretend
to be wise above what is there written. . . . "

The attitude toward the Bible, however, is not con-
sistent. On the one hand we find its authority fully
acknowledged; it is even taken as the guide in all temporal
affairs.[20] On the other hand the principle is laid down:
"The Spirit is that guide by which the saints are led into

[18] Fox reproaches the other churches with holding a theory of worship
which is the reverse of the true one; experience of the Divine, he says,
proceeds from form to content, from man to Christ, whereas in the
church the direction is from the spirit to ritual, from content to form,
from Christ to man. A modern Quaker, Samuel Tuke, justifies the rejection of ritual as follows: "The contest for Judaical rites in the Christian
Church, is as if a man were determined, when his house was built, to
keep up the scaffolding—to be more careful of *its* preservation, than of
the *structure* for the service of which it was erected." *Samuel Tuke, his
Life, Work and Thoughts,* edited by Charles Tylor, London 1900, p. 266.
[19] *Book of Christian Discipline of the Religious Society of Friends,*
London 1883, p. 56: hereafter referred to as *Discipline.*
[20] "The least doubt touching the truth of the Holy Scriptures poisons
the heart and lays the foundation for the greatest evils."

all Truth; therefore, according to the scriptures, the Spirit is the first and principal leader." "The Spirit and not the scriptures is the rule"; [21] and it may be counted as one of the advantages of Quaker doctrine that it puts personal experience above the revelations of history, and thus evades the difficulty arising from the conflict of many Biblical statements with science and history.[22]

In order not to check the development of religion corresponding to the increasing insight of mankind, their doctrine is not laid down in any confession of faith binding for all time; [23] certain writings, to be specified later, dating from the years 1650 to 1680, are evidently very influential but are not regarded as official declarations; nor is even Barclay's *Apology* so considered.

The disapproval of traditional forms which led to Divine service without a set ritual resulted also in the failure to use the sacraments and the ancient forms of prayer. "Sacraments," their doctrine holds, "cannot be traced back to ancient Jewish practices, but are to be compared with heathen cults and rites." [24] As an argument against the ceremony of baptism may be urged the frequent inability of the godfathers to perform what they promise. Not having any priests, the Quakers naturally dispensed with

[21] Robert Barclay, *An Apology for the True Christian Divinity* (published in Latin in 1676; 1st English edition 1678), 8th edition London 1780, pp. 67, 68, 72. In this connection see also Hylkema, *op. cit.*: "The Scriptures are not the light, but a witness to the Light."

[22] John William Graham: "The revelation of God in science and history is our delight": in *The Meaning of Quakerism*, London n.d., p. 45.

[23] Penn: "The New Testament alone is our creed and that reserves liberty of interpretation to the reader."

[24] Matthias Schneckenburger, *Vorlesungen über die Lehrbegriffe der kleineren protestantischen Kirchenparteien* (Lectures on the doctrines of the smaller Protestant churches), Frankfurt am Main 1863, p. 69ff.

the official benediction at marriages [25] and recognized no need for the assistance of the church at burials in the traditional way, even though, as will be shown later,[26] they did take part, in a semi-official capacity, in these functions, and kept official records of them.

In continuing the account of the negative aspects of Quakerism, we may mention their refusal to take or administer oaths,[27] resulting from obedience to the Biblical prohibition, and their refusal to bear arms, because of the many evils which arise from war.[28] Fox even proposed the institution of a European court of justice, and Penn worked the plan out in some detail.[29] The Quakers recognize, to be sure, that men may fight in cases in which it seems to them personally justifiable to do so; but whoever does not share this view (as must always be the case among the Quakers themselves as a consequence of their teaching) ought not to be compelled to fight.[30]

We may refer lastly to their habit of dispensing with

[25] See below, p. 41.

[26] God, in the Quakers' view, is the one who makes marriages; therefore marriages cannot be solemnized by officials or priests.

[27] Affirmation, or solemn promise, in place of an oath was permitted in 1689 through the Act of Toleration.

[28] *Discipline*, p. 157: "The whole life and teaching of our Lord and Saviour is one continued testimony against the spirit of war. His words are not to be annulled by the teachings of men. We look with serious apprehension upon the existence and increase of military centres. How often do they become also centres of demoralisation and sin!"

[29] *An Essay towards the Present and Future Peace of Europe by the Establishment of an European Dyet, Parlament or Estates*, Beati Pacifici 1693: attributed to William Penn. Reprinted in *Old South Leaflets*, vol. iii, No. 75.

[30] The Quakers have been reproached with lack of patriotism because of their refusal to bear arms. They defend themselves against this charge by explaining that the Christian conception of patriotism is not the same as the Jewish and heathen conception, for the latter derived from the idea of a tribal God, who loved Palestine but cursed Edom.

certain forms of conventional politeness in speech and behavior, their refusal to use misleading expressions of address and certain expressions of heathen origin (as for example the plural form *you* as the pronoun of address for one person, and the names of the months and of days of the week), and to their injunction not to dress in the fashionable clothing of the time.[31] The equal worth of all men, in Fox's view, did not permit markedly courteous or deferential behavior to the few, or the practice of raising one's hat to them. In the refusal of Fox and his followers to observe the contemporary custom in this respect there was also a protest against the spirit of servility which had been on the increase in England since the days of Queen Elizabeth; just as the simple dress (which ultimately became in effect a special uniform, because it did not change with the passing years) constituted a testimony against the exaggeratedly extravagant clothing of the time. It was a common saying that the toilet of a lady was more laborious and time-consuming than the rigging of a warship.

The negative side of Quakerism was at first more striking than the positive side. The contributions of the movement that were new and valuable naturally did not come to light until the Society had developed somewhat. Fox set up one fundamental requirement, that men should follow without question the leadings of the Inner Light, and thus give reality to the Kingdom of God even in this life. In contrast to the gloomy doctrine of predestination, Fox

[31] See *No Cross, No Crown, or several sober reasons against Hat-Honor, Titular Respects, You to a single person, with the Apparel and Recreations of the Times, etc.,* by W. Penn jun. An humble Disciple, and patient Bearer of the Cross of Jesus. Printed in 1669; often reprinted.

taught that the love of God is not limited to a small circle of the elect, but that Christ died for the sins of the whole world. He did not therefore regard himself in any sense as the founder of a new denomination; according to his unalterable conviction, all Christendom, and indeed ultimately all humanity, would have to become Children of the Light. (This view, to be sure, was held by the members of many other sects.) When confronted by the Truth which he had brought to light, and which he considered to be identical with the revelations given to the primitive Christians, all the differences in faith, arising from human stupidity or perhaps from the personal interest of the clergy, completely lost their significance. There resulted therefore a certain degree of toleration, even for the Roman Catholics; though this toleration extended only to their laity, purposely kept in ignorance, while Fox fought vigorously against the clergy and such temporal officers as were connected with church affairs.[32]

This toleration, however, did not by any means indicate that any leniency should be evidenced to one's own brethren in the Quaker faith. Backsliding into sinfulness seemed impossible for one who had once seen the true Light. Catholics as well as Lutherans take into account the weakness and sinful nature of man—confession and communion can always be used to effect a return to grace; but in all the reformed sects, those elected by God to salvation must keep themselves pure of sin, in order to attain to their salvation. Even though the Quakers, as men-

[32] "The union of the Church with the State derives no support from the New Testament." *Discipline,* p. 142.

tioned above, do entirely reject the doctrine of predestination, still when the Inner Light breaks upon them they find themselves in much the situation that Calvin ascribes to the elect, and hence have the capability, and the obligation, to lead a pure life.[33] It is true that they cannot altogether escape temptations, and they should be constantly on guard against a worldly spirit,[34] which must be combated by prayer, religious meditation, and Bible reading, and kept in its proper place by avoidance of diversions, reading, and conversation of a worldly nature.[35] For each year a set of Queries is propounded to Quakers for the earnest testing of their religious condition, which until quite recently have been answered in writing.

Justification can be attained through both prayer and good works, in reference to which the Quakers occupy a middle position between the Catholics and the great Protestant churches. In Barclay's view, works cannot be left out in a consideration of justification. He says, in the *Apology* (p. 205): "We understand not by this [expression] 'justification by Christ' barely the good works even wrought by the Spirit of Christ; for they, as Protestants truly affirm, are rather an effect of justification than the cause of it; but we understand the *formation of Christ in us, Christ born and brought forth in us,* from which good works as naturally proceed as fruit from a fruitful tree. It is this inward birth in us, bringing forth righteousness and holiness in us, that doth justify us." Further

[33] Barclay, *Apology*, p. 145ff.

[34] See for example *Epistles from the Yearly Meeting of Friends held in London,* 2 vols. London 1858, (hereafter referred to as *Yearly Meeting Epistles*), 1, 92 (for the year 1698).

[35] *Discipline,* p. 46: "Much hurt may accrue to the religious mind by long and frequent conversation on temporal matters."

(p. 207): "We believe that such works as naturally proceed from this spiritual birth and formation of Christ in us are pure and holy, even as the root from which they come; and therefore God accepts them, and justifies us in them and rewards us for them out of his own free grace." Further (p. 208): "Since good works as naturally follow from this birth as heat from fire, therefore are they of absolute necessity to justification." In these words we have the union of the mystical with the practical, a characteristic of the Quakers. Their ideal is not silent absorption in God to the neglect of temporal affairs, but glorification of God in this present world through devotion to the obligations which he has imposed.[26]

It was to be expected that the spread of Quakerism, conflicting as it did with many traditional views, would be marked by troubles. For a while, to be sure, the complete confusion that prevailed in the established order in church and state when Fox made his first appearance as a traveling preacher made it possible for him to gather together a considerable number of adherents without being interfered with. Fox, however, did not rest content with the peaceful dissemination of his religious experiences, but, stirred by indignation at the clergy, whose lives were often not above reproach, he began aggressive attacks upon established churches.

Custom in those days permitted laymen to speak to the congregation after the sermon had been finished; and Fox used this opportunity to heap reproaches upon "the hire-

---

[26] An interesting account of early Quakerism is contained in *Reliquiae Baxterianae or Mr. Richard Baxter's Narrative of the most Memorable Passages of his Life and Times*. Faithfully published from his own Original Manuscript by Matthew Sylvester, London 1696, p. 77ff.

lings who waxed fat upon the tithes of the people." Imprisonment often resulted; but after the jail term had been served, he would renew the polemic, and again be thrown into jail. Fox's Journal is full of accounts of longer or shorter imprisonments in different parts of the country. So long as he enjoyed freedom he worked vigorously at increasing the number of his followers. He tells us himself that he often spoke for three hours before immense gatherings, and that some of the independent clergymen voluntarily turned over their churches to him [37] and were much moved by his words.

By 1652 there were regular meetings of Quakers in Lancashire and neighboring districts. Fox himself took up his residence about this time in Swarthmore Hall, the estate of a certain Judge Fell, whose friendship protected him from the fury of the clergy, and who permitted him to make Swarthmore Hall the headquarters of the whole movement. [38] From here he sent out traveling ministers [39]

[37] The church buildings themselves Fox called "steeple-houses." The "church" was for him only the community of believers. See his definition in the *Journal*, i, 25 and *passim*.

[38] After Fell's death in 1658 his widow Margaret Fell and the Quakers who met at her house had a great deal of persecution to endure. In 1669 Fox married Margaret Fell, after seeing to it that her property should descend to the children of her first marriage. Fox wished for no material advantage for himself from this alliance (*Journal*, ii, 117, 118); nevertheless Margaret Fell did a great deal for the Society with her money. The labors in which they both engaged toward spreading the faith, and the frequent confinements in prison, made it impossible for them to live together except at rare intervals. Margaret Fox died in 1702 in her eighty-eighth year.

[39] The term "minister" is used by Quakers to mean any member of the Society who, feeling himself especially called to proclaim the Word of God, and speaking more or less frequently, and acceptably, in the meetings for worship, has been officially recognized by the meeting as a minister. Such persons are called "recorded ministers," as opposed to the "ordained ministers" of other churches.

to all parts of the country for the systematic dissemination of the new doctrine.

The followers of these preachers called themselves at first "Children of the Light," then "Friends of Truth," and finally "Society of Friends"; this last is still the official designation. With regard to the origin of the name "Quaker" (that is, "trembler"), which is far better known in Germany, opinion is divided. Fox himself says that Judge Bennet in Derby called him by this name, in 1650, because Fox summoned him to tremble before the word of God.[40] The designation may also come from the fact that some of Fox's first followers fell into a state of extreme religious excitement, or fasted till they became hysterical from exhaustion, and were seized with convulsions, during which, it is said, the Inner Light shone in upon them. Occasionally, too, they tore their clothes from their bodies [41] in symbolic representation of their spiritual rebirth; but such excesses occurred in even greater degree [42] among the Enthusiasts, and the reports may have been exaggerated through malice. At any rate it may be assumed that Fox and the majority of the

[40] *Journal*, i, 58.

[41] In this connection see chapter on *Going Naked a Sign* in *First Publishers of Truth, Being Early Records of the Introduction of Quakerism . . .*, edited by Norman Penney, London 1907, p. 364ff. An account is given there of how the "Spirit" demanded this as a sign and miracle for the unbelievers, and often brought the few who would have liked to escape this sacrifice into great need and distress. See also pp. 71, 213, 259, etc.; also *A Collection of the Sufferings of the People called Quakers . . . Taken from Original Records and other Authentic Accounts*, by Joseph Besse (hereafter referred to as Besse's *Sufferings*) 1753, i, 393; and William Simpson's pamphlet, *Going Naked, a Signe*, London 1660.

[42] By way of example, mention may be made of the extravagances of John Robins, John Reeve, and Lodowicke Muggleton. See W. Godwin, *History of the Commonwealth of England*, London 1824, iv, 313ff.

BRIEF OUTLINE OF THE QUAKER MOVEMENT

Quaker preachers knew how to lead their hearers back to sanity. Their extravagant language, however strange it appears to us, was the customary manner of speech among religious people in the middle and lower classes,[43] and from these classes, especially in the rural districts, the Quaker following was recruited. Even among the soldiers of Cromwell's army, in which there was a high degree of religious fervor, there were numerous Quakers.

It was different in London. Fox's disciple James Nayler had a distinguished congregation there; members of the most exclusive society (for instance, Sir Henry Vane) attended his services, though sometimes incognito. This external success, however, was probably the occasion of an occurrence which might easily have brought incalculable harm to the movement. In 1656 Nayler had himself proclaimed in the streets of Bristol as King of Israel, and accepted the homage of a small group of fanatically enthusiastic people, who went about with him calling out "Hosanna," until the authorities put an end to the disturbance.

Naturally this situation gave the opponents of Quakerism a welcome opportunity to attack them, though the Quakers immediately disclaimed Nayler and did not receive him back into fellowship until long afterwards, when he had admitted his error and done suitable penance. Although many of Nayler's admirers interceded for him, he did not escape a terrible punishment: Cromwell granted no pardons in cases of blasphemy. Pillory, scourging, boring through the tongue, and designation of the kind of crime by branding the letter B (for "blasphemy") on the

[43] Barclay, *The Inner Life,* p. 214.

forehead were the usual punishments in those days, and perhaps necessary as a means of terrifying the rough and uneducated masses, who tended all too easily to go to extremes.[44]

The tragedy of Nayler did not fail to exercise a wholesome influence on other Quaker preachers. For the dream of the realization of the Kingdom of God on earth stirred many to resist the public authorities,[45] though the significance and danger of such resistance was probably overestimated.[46] The general opinion about them can be gathered, for instance, from a letter of Henry Cromwell, who wrote to John Thurloe, Secretary of the Council of State, in 1655: "Our most considerable enemy now in our view are the quakers. . . . Their counterfeited simplicitie renders them to me the more dangerous." [47] Many of the clergy, too, believed that the Quakers would soon progress to the point of a general orgy of butchering, and they were occasionally impelled by fear to call upon the people to defend themselves.

This was a groundless fear: Fox was a vigorous fighter, but only for his faith. He took almost no interest in politics. Only one thing roused him to opposition: the desire of Cromwell to assume the crown. The Protector satis-

[44] Barclay, *The Inner Life,* p. 216: "The air was thick with reports of prophecies and miracles, and there were men of all parties who lived on the border land between sanity and insanity."

[45] Another reason for such resistance lay in the fact that the Quakers, as evidenced for instance in a petition addressed to Cromwell, looked upon *all* persecution as unjustifiable, since the laws penalizing failure to belong to the Established Church were no longer in force.

[46] According to estimates made by the Quakers themselves, more than 3,000 of their members were thrown into prison on account of disturbance of the peace during the years 1656-58.

[47] *A Collection of the State Papers of John Thurloe, Esq. . . . ,* in 7 vols., by Thomas Birch, London 1742, iv, 508.

fied himself of Fox's peaceful views through a personal interview, and thereafter he was always well disposed toward him.[48] After Cromwell's death, and especially after the resignation of Richard Cromwell, the chaotic conditions of England again stimulated the fanatical zeal of the religious sects; but this last climax of the Reformation was followed, after the return of Charles II in May, 1660, by a sudden collapse. Not only were Independents and Enthusiasts entirely deprived of political rights again; even the Presbyterians, to whose coöperation the Restoration practically owed its success, found themselves tolerated for only a short time. The Corporation Act of January, 1661, prepared the way for uniformity, for by this means the qualification for all offices was made to depend upon membership in the Episcopal Church; and this Church, after the failure of the Savoy Conference, was again elevated, in May of the next year, to the position of the only officially recognized church. Within a short time clergymen, teachers, members of university faculties, and other officials, had to subscribe to a declaration of conformity, or lose their positions. How much distress and misery came through this requirement to many worthy men and their families,[49] and at the same time what repercussions there were in the lives of the people!

The Puritans had protested against the frivolity of the

[48] There were four meetings between the first Quaker and Cromwell during the years 1654-58.

[49] According to Macaulay, "about two thousand of the ministers of religion, whose conscience did not suffer them to conform, were driven from their benefices in one day." Thomas B. Macaulay, *The History of England,* 5 vols., Boston 1856, i, 137. In this connection see further Baxter, *op. cit.,* pp. 384, 385.

upper classes ever since the time of James I; and public opinion had been influenced in very large measure by their strict morality. Religion in the sense of Calvinistic piety had been the watchword of the time—we may refer in passing to the widespread animosity which had been caused by the publication of the so-called "Book of Sports"; [50] and now the court and its hangers-on presented a picture of moral degeneration which was mitigated by neither beauty nor grace,[51] and which was extensively imitated by the masses—and more so as decency and religious observance not only brought mockery and scorn, but even the suspicion of treasonable activity. The Nonconformists, as the Presbyterians, Independents, Anabaptists, and Quakers were called after the publication of the Act of Uniformity, soon acquired the reputation of being "melancholy fanatics, who darken the smiling heaven of life with their gloomy asceticism, and, as they are unable to enjoy social pleasures themselves, try to keep others from taking part in them." Petitions for tolerance, accompanied by reference to the Declaration of Breda,[52] were answered with empty promises; by means of the strictest persecution the authorities attempted to force the people into conformity. The testimony of one person was enough to bring down punishment upon anyone suspected; and this regulation engendered an odious

[50] *A Declaration to encourage recreations and the sports on the Lord's Day,* May 24, 1618. See Neal, *op. cit.,* i, 472; ii, 200; also Gardiner, *Constitutional Documents,* p. 99.

[51] Neal, *op. cit.,* iii, 107.

[52] A statement issued by Charles II in 1660 assuring amnesty to all except those especially excluded by Parliament, and promising liberty to tender consciences in matters of religion not contrary to the peace of the kingdom.

swarm of talebearers, as under earlier rulers, who fat-
tened themselves on the possessions of their victims while
the latter pined away in prison. Under the last Stuarts, at
least 12,000 Quakers suffered severe prison sentences, as
a result of which more than 300 died.[53] And when all
the adult members of a congregation were languishing in
prison, the children often continued the meetings in the
open air. Their youth protected them from imprisonment, but not from cruel punishment. But this very oppression had an effect of winning adherents to the cause
of the Quakers which must not be underestimated: not
only persons who paid no attention to official prohibitions
because they had nothing to lose, but also many who belonged to the substantial middle class[54] threw their lot
in with them during this period.

Weingarten and other church historians distinguish a
second period of the Quaker movement which began with
the Restoration; and, indeed, its character did change
with the political and social conditions. In place of
the Puritan's zeal for reforming all England, or even perhaps the whole world,[55] which stuck at nothing, there
arose a widespread tendency toward withdrawal into a
defensive attitude, and concentration upon the building
up of the Society. From the beginning the Quakers had
felt themselves to be like a great family, and had assembled not only for worship but for mutual help and

[53] For detailed accounts see Besse's *Sufferings;* Sewel's *History;* Fox's
Journal, i, 493, ii, 252, etc.; William Beck, *George Whitehead, His Work
and Service,* London 1901; etc., etc.
[54] According to Barclay, *The Inner Life,* p. 350, the London meetings
alone had more than 10,000 members in 1678.
[55] The zeal of the first Quakers in making converts was compared
with that of the Jesuits.

advice. Mention is made of this practice from 1653 on; but the assemblies did not become regular until after the Restoration. Whether this is to be ascribed to Fox or, as Weingarten assumes, to the London Quakers, is not of interest here. We may merely mention that, in addition to the meetings for worship held on "the first day of the week," [56] the congregations began to hold monthly meetings embracing, for the time being, all the members within a given district; that from these in turn delegates were sent to a quarterly meeting covering a specific district of larger extent; and that finally there was held a Yearly Meeting in London, composed of representatives sent by the quarterly meetings,[57] and forming the ultimate authority in the affairs of all Quakers in England.

The functions of these meetings were not very clearly defined in the earliest days, but have now become fairly well settled. The monthly meeting [58] acts in the matter of taking in new members; gives to members who move out of any given district a certificate of membership to take to other congregations; and appoints elders, who watch over the private life of the ministers in particular, but also of all members individually, attempting to persuade any erring members to mend their ways, or effecting their expulsion. Further, the monthly meeting appoints overseers, who assist the elders in their duties and sit in

[56] The "first day of the week" (Sunday) is not regarded as being especially holy, though the Quakers refrain from carrying on their business on that day, following the example of the first Christians. "All days are alike holy in the sight of God" (Barclay, *Apology,* p. 349); therefore they do not favor a "superstitious" observance of feast days and holy days.
[57] This meeting, unlike the quarterly meeting, was not open to the members in general, until about the middle of the nineteenth century.
[58] *Discipline,* p. 193ff.

with them in the Meetings on Ministry and Oversight. Approval of proposed marriages also is granted in the monthly meeting, after it has ascertained that no hindrances intervene. When the approval has been expressed, and not until then, betrothed couples may consummate the ceremony of appearing before a meeting for worship and solemnly announcing their intention of belonging to each other as man and wife; whereupon the marriage is considered accomplished,[59] and is recorded by the Society.[60]

At the quarterly meeting,[61] reports are read from the monthly meetings within the jurisdiction, and any matters of disagreement are discussed. In case a member feels dissatisfaction with the decision of a monthly meeting, he can appeal to the higher authority of the quarterly meeting, or even from it to the Yearly Meeting. The Yearly Meeting bears the same relation to the quarterly meeting as each quarterly meeting to its constituent monthly meetings. There is no presiding officer in any of the meetings; a clerk, however, is appointed to record the decisions, for the purpose of notifying members regarding them. It is interesting that there is no voting. If agreement cannot be reached on a given matter, consideration of it is postponed, sometimes until the next meeting; the result is finally minuted as the joint will of the whole congregation, the "sense of the meeting."

From the need of having in the Society some agency,

[59] In 1656 Cromwell had introduced civil marriage with a similar ceremony. The declaration of the bridal couple was confirmed in such cases by a justice.

[60] An act of Queen Victoria (10 & 11 Vict. c. 58) declared all the earlier Quaker marriages solemnized in this way to be legally valid.

[61] *Discipline,* p. 188ff.

meeting oftener than once a year, that could act authoritatively in important matters of general concern, there arose in course of time various committees of the Yearly Meeting, whose members were limited in numbers and appointed by the Yearly Meeting. The best known of these is the Meeting for Sufferings. Women take part on an equal footing with men in the ministry [62] and in all meetings.[63] In Quaker circles it is believed that a very considerable influence was exerted upon the character of women in general, not only within the Society, but indirectly far beyond its limits, through the complete recognition of women as helpers in spiritual and temporal matters.[64]

Various writings have come down to us with regard to the guiding principles of Quakerism from the years during which it was assuming definite form, such as the *Apology* (1676) of Robert Barclay, already mentioned, the so-called *Canons and Institutions* [65] of George Fox, John Crook's *Truth's Principles* (1663), and Edward Burrough's *A Declaration to all the World of our Faith* (1657). Translations, principally into Dutch, but also into German, French, and even Spanish, brought about

[62] We hear of Quaker women preachers as early as 1650. "Elizabeth Hooton was among the earliest exponents of Quakerism, perhaps the earliest next to George Fox." *First Publishers of Truth,* p. 219, *note.*

[63] J. P. Gooch, *History of the English Democratic Ideas in the Seventeenth Century,* Cambridge Historical Essays, No. 10, 1898, p. 272, *note:* "So prominent was the position occupied by women among the Quakers that it was at first rumoured that the sect was confined to the female sex."

[64] *Discipline,* p. 218.

[65] A document believed to have been written in 1668, first printed in 1669; reprinted in William Beck and T. Frederick Ball, *The London Friends' Meetings,* London 1869 (hereafter referred to as Beck and Ball), pp. 47-52.

extensive dissemination of its doctrines, and rounded out the oral preaching done by missionaries. In a circular letter of 1660 it is stated that various places in Italy, France, Switzerland, and Norway had been visited, as well as Turkey, Palestine, Virginia, Newfoundland, Barbados, Bermuda, Jamaica, and Surinam.[66]

The missionary activity of the Quakers was, and is, directed less toward winning members for their Society (for relatively few persons can meet the exacting demands of the Quakers in the matter of religious and moral life), than toward disseminating Christian ideas in general.[67] The result of this fact was that for two hundred and fifty years no Quaker settlements worthy of the name arose except in the Anglo-Saxon nations. (A revival of missionary enterprise and the dissemination of Quaker influence since the World War have given rise in recent years to the formation of Quaker communities in other parts of the world.) The importance of the Society in America is essentially due to William Penn, who thus deserves the title of second founder of Quakerism.[68]

[66] In connection with Quaker preachers in Holland see Hylkema, *op. cit.* (see note 14), pp. 47-72.

[67] The original Quakers to be sure made no such distinction; for them the Quaker doctrine was the Gospel pure and simple—and no other gospel would do.

[68] For estimates of Penn see William Hepworth Dixon, *William Penn, an Historical Biography,* London 1851, and the German translation, with revisions, by Ernst Bunsen, under the title *William Penn oder die Zustände Englands 1644 bis 1718* (William Penn, or conditions in England from 1644 to 1718), Leipzig 1854; Allen C. and Richard H. Thomas, *History of the Society of Friends in America,* 6th edition Philadelphia 1930; Isaac Sharpless, *A Quaker Experiment in Government,* Philadelphia 1898; John W. Graham, *William Penn, Founder of Pennsylvania,* London 1916; Mabel R. Brailsford, *The Making of William Penn,* London 1930.

The ancestry of this second founder offers a sharp contrast to Fox's modest birth. Penn was the son (born 1644) of William Penn (afterwards Admiral Penn), who, though in the service of the Commonwealth, entered into intrigues in the interests of the Stuarts, and was appropriately rewarded by them in various ways. The son did not share the father's liking for court life; even during his university days he protested, with other students, against Charles II's introduction of Catholic practices, and neglected to attend the high-church services, though attendance was required. He felt himself moreover much drawn by the sermons of a layman, Thomas Loe, who was proclaiming Fox's teachings.

The Admiral, by no means approving his son's tendencies, which led to his expulsion from the University, hoped to bring about a change of heart by sending him for a stay in France; but the change lasted only a short while. After William Penn's return the Plague broke out in England (in 1665), and this terrible visitation made a lasting impression on him. Again it appeared necessary to the Admiral to divert his son's mind, so he sent him to Ireland to the court of the viceroy, the Duke of Ormonde. There, however, Penn met Thomas Loe again, and also came into contact with a number of his fellow believers, and soon became himself a convinced Quaker.

In Ireland the Quakers were especially despised and persecuted; Penn himself did not escape. At first to be sure his father demanded his release, but disowned him when William refused to give up his new faith. In spite of repeated imprisonments he worked at the spreading of the Quaker doctrine by preaching and writing. In 1670 he fell a victim to the Conventicle Act; [69] the suit in the Old Bailey against him and William Meade is famous. For the jurors refused to find the accused guilty, although they were repeatedly punished with fines and even locked up until the Lord Mayor effected their release.[70]

Soon after this Penn lost his father, who had been reconciled to him before his death, and had even procured for him the special favor of the Duke of York. Under such circumstances it became possible for Penn to be useful to his brothers in the faith in many ways; and he was finally even able to establish a colony which served as a safe place of refuge on the other side of the ocean for the persecuted Quakers of England.[71] This colony brought to fruition a plan that had long been cherished by Fox. There were already little settlements of Quaker fugitives on the banks of the Delaware River,[72] and Fox and Penn had been there for visits of some little duration. Admiral Penn had advanced considerable sums of money to the royal treasury, and instead of repayment the son requested a grant of uncolonized crown land in

[69] In 16 Car. II. c. 4 (1664), gatherings are forbidden of more than five persons not belonging to the same family, if for the purpose of religious exercise according to any rites other than those of the Established Church. Fine and imprisonment for first and second offenses were followed by transportation for seven years in case of a third offense.

[70] John Fiske, *The Dutch and Quaker Colonies in America,* Boston and New York 1899, ii, 129, compares this trial with the Dreyfus case.

[71] Even though the last of the Stuarts was kindly disposed toward the Quakers—after his ascent of the throne he gave 1,200 Quaker prisoners their liberty—they were still persecuted by public officials as well as by the Catholics.

[72] In the colonies of other English Puritans, with the exception of Rhode Island, Quakers were not tolerated. Most of the communities of those who had fled from England treated persons whose faith was different from their own with the same intolerance which they had themselves suffered from.

America.[73] He received a tract of 45,000 square miles
lying north of Maryland and west of New Jersey—almost
as much area as all England. In March, 1680, the deed
was delivered to him; the name "Pennsylvania" was given
to the land, and the royal privileges regulated.

With the assistance of Algernon Sydney, Penn worked
out a constitution which gave the sovereignty to the people. Numerous agents from England and from the lower
Rhine valley were soon arranging with Penn about the
purchase of tracts of this land, which Penn had received
by deed from Charles II, and had then acquired from
the aboriginal Indian inhabitants by peaceful purchase.
In the course of three years, 7,000 persons had settled
there, and the new colony prospered beyond expectation.[74]

The founder himself had many bitter disappointments
to endure. In order to represent the interests of the colony
before the King, who would have preferred to recover
the colony for himself, Penn found it necessary
to return, and in his absence the colonists fell to quarreling. Penn to be sure succeeded in quieting the disturbance; but after his death (in 1718) his incompetent sons
were not able permanently to maintain themselves in the
position of dominance. The leadership of the popular
assembly at least remained in the hands of the Quakers,
until the outbreak of the American Revolutionary War

[73] According to David Macpherson, *Annals of Commerce, Manufactures, Fisheries, and Navigation,* London 1805, ii, 598, Admiral Penn had
assured himself of the granting to him of land in America before he
died.

[74] See Thomas, Sharpless, and Fiske (notes 68 and 70); see also
James Bowden, *The History of the Society of Friends in America,* London 1850-54, and Rufus M. Jones, *The Quakers in the American Colonies,* London 1911.

forced them on religious grounds to withdraw from politics. In later times they restricted their activity to their own organization, and formed a closed social group, just as in England, which hardly took part in public affairs.

With Penn passed away the greatest of the Quakers who had had personal relations with Fox. The latter had died in 1691 without issue. The end of his life marked the high tide of the Quaker movement in England—the number of Quakers was estimated at this time at 70,000 to 80,000; shortly afterwards the movement suffered a considerable setback. This is partially to be ascribed to the natural reaction which occurred in religious matters all over England after the Toleration Act of 1689. There were indeed traveling preachers who disseminated their ideas with great candor at almost all the courts of Europe; but they were isolated instances—the Society as a whole retired into itself, in order to live a sober, serious life far from the "temptations of the world," taking anxious care to maintain the requirements of the Discipline of their forefathers down to the smallest details.

After the religious awakening in England effected by the Methodists, a gradual revival took place among the Quakers too, which first showed itself in philanthropic activity. Missionary zeal did not come to the fore until within the last fifty years, and, in America, was felt in only one group of Quakers. For among American Friends serious disagreements had broken out in 1827, leading ultimately to a separation into four parties,[75]

[75] The first separation resulted in two parties, the Orthodox and Hicksites. The Wilburites and the Primitive Friends arose later.

whose views and objectives differed from each other in important details. Even among the English Quakers, there are, properly speaking, three groups [76] to be distinguished, although peaceful coöperation is not interfered with. On the contrary, there is an earnest, and successful effort being made to prevent further separation and reduction of membership; [77] and on this account the principal cause of the loss of members, i.e., the prohibition of marriage with non-Quakers, was done away with in 1860. Even before this the repeal of the Test and Corporation Acts had made it possible for the Quakers to hold municipal offices (1829) and to enter Parliament (1833); and since they have ceased in latter days to require certain usages which now serve no purpose (as in the matter of the plain dress and language), a further bar has fallen, which formerly tended to differentiate the Quakers from other citizens.

Whether their more important ideas will experience a further expansion, as they themselves hope, or whether there is taking place a process of absorption of their membership, which now numbers only about 19,000 in England and Wales, only the future will show. [78] The con-

[76] According to Edward Grubb, *Quakerism in England: its Present Position*, London 1901, pp. 18-23, three elements can be distinguished, the conservative, the evangelical, and the intellectual. One group composed mainly of evangelically inclined members withdrew and now are a constituent part of the Plymouth Brethren.

[77] The increase by the birth of children to members is less than the decrease by death; on the other hand, the increase by taking in new members is greater than the decrease by the loss of living members. See Grubb, *op. cit.*, p. 3.

[78] In addition to the above we must reckon about 9,000 "habitual attenders and associates." In America there are further about 100,000 Quakers, in other lands about 1,000.

servatism of the Quakers in matters of doctrine, and the spiritual tendency of our time, make it seem likely that new members will be won not so much by their doctrine in itself as by its realization in the social life of the Society.

CHAPTER ONE

POOR RELIEF

BEFORE we begin our discussion of the social and humanitarian work of the Quakers, a brief review of the economic condition of England in the middle of the seventeenth century is essential. In our introductory remarks on the religious and political situation at the time of the rise of the Quakers, a brief sketch of the period of the Reformation down to Cromwell was sufficient; but in the present connection it seems necessary to examine rather closely the whole eventful period, extending from the reign of Henry VIII down to about the time of the outbreak of the Civil War. Rogers [1] states that he has found very few reliable reports regarding this epoch, and he rejects the undocumented statements of other historians with regard to its prosperity. By comparing wages, rents exacted from tenant farmers, and prices, he comes to the conclusion, however, that it was a period of extraordinary misery for the great mass of the people and for the tenant farmers—a time in which few were able to get rich, while many sank into hopeless poverty.

The causes are manifold. The rise of large-scale agriculture at the close of the Middle Ages was one of these causes. Between 1470 and 1530 the first great inclosures

[1] Thorold Rogers, *Economic Interpretation of History,* New York 1889, p. 139ff.

of grazing land had been made—that is, much of the pasturage which had till then been open for common grazing was transformed into private property, and at the same time the right of the common use of land, and the common-field system of agriculture,[2] was abolished. In a pamphlet from the year 1581[3] the complaint is voiced: "and wheare xl persons had theire lyvinges, nowe one man and his shepard hath all. Which thinge is not the least cause of theise vprors [i.e., uproars], for by theise inclosures men doe lacke lyvinges and be idle . . . Moreover, all thinges are so deare that by theire daily labour they are not able to live."

The famine in the sixteenth century is attributed in this pamphlet to the debasement of the coinage effected by Henry VIII; for, according to Rogers, the value of English money in foreign countries dropped to one fifth of its face value as a result of this debasement. Later the granting of monopolies for most of the articles of daily consumption[4] and the concentration of trade in the hands

[2] In the village community, the land was divided into arable land, meadow, pasture, and waste. The arable land was divided into two or three fields, which were cut up into strips and allotted to the villagers in such a way that one holding might include several disconnected strips in each field—a measure designed to prevent the whole of the best land from falling to one man. Such division and use of the arable land constituted the common-field system of agriculture.

[3] *A Discourse of the Common Weal of the Realm of England*, edited from the MSS by Elizabeth Lamond, Cambridge 1893. First printed in 1581 under title: *A compendious or briefe examination of certayne ordinary complaints, of diuers of our country men* . . . By W. S., Gentleman. This book is often ascribed to William Stafford, but is more probably by John Hales.

[4] The poverty of the crown as a result of the boundless extravagance of Henry VIII compelled Elizabeth, James I, and Charles I to adopt such means of raising money. There was moreover this great evil, that the enormous profits of the middlemen bore no sort of proportion to the contributions which they made to the royal treasury.

of about 200 persons [5] were especially effective in raising the cost of living. At the same time wages were depressed, for in the sixteenth century home industry encroached upon regular trade, and the medieval scheme of city government went to pieces with the decline of the guilds,[6] so that the entire established economic order crumbled. To be sure, Article xv of the so-called Apprentice Law of Queen Elizabeth [7] decreed that wages should be fixed annually by a justice of the peace acting jointly with sheriff and city authorities, and in consultation with experts, but this article had to do with maximum wages; [8] and in the process of standardizing wages little attention was paid to variations in the prices of the means of subsistence. Rogers makes an estimate of the minimum cost of living, and states that the average laborer between 1583 and 1623 could make only 73 per cent of this minimum, and between 1628 and 1663 about 82 to 84 per cent.[9]

[5] See W. A. S. Hewins, *English Trade and Finance, chiefly in the Seventeenth Century*, London 1892, p. 30.

[6] The power of the guilds was restricted by the Duke of Somerset, as Protector, and a large class of the population was thus deprived of support in time of distress. See Arnold Toynbee, *Lectures on the Industrial Revolution of the Eighteenth Century in England*, 3d edition London 1890, p. 98.

[7] *An Act touching divers orders of Artificers, Labourers, Servants of Husbandry, and Apprentices*, 5 Eliz. c. 4, consisting of forty-eight articles. See Sir George Nicholls, *A History of the English Poor Law*, London 1854, i, 157.

[8] The payment of higher wages was punished by fine and imprisonment; the acceptance of higher wages by imprisonment for a lengthy term. See Adolf Held, *Zwei Bücher zur sozialen Geschichte Englands* (Two books on the social history of England), Leipzig 1881.

[9] In the north of England the nominal wages were about 50% lower than in the regions studied, the real wages about 35—40% lower.

Wages were everywhere lowest in agriculture,[10] so that among country people it soon became customary to engage in spinning wool as a secondary occupation. On this account the wool industry, which was primarily concerned with weaving cloth, became dependent upon agriculture; so that the weavers suffered a shortage of raw material during the harvest time. As a general thing industrial workers could count upon work for 200 to 260 days during a year; and those whose income needed augmenting even during the time when they could get work, inevitably found that during the time of enforced idleness, amounting to about a third of the year, they became totally dependent upon the community, and increased the already large number of those who were continuously supported by public funds. This applies especially to the successors of that wandering class, too lazy or too incompetent to work, which had been brought into existence by the indiscriminate almsgiving of the convents, and which, after the ecclesiastical properties had been confiscated by Henry VIII, constituted a veritable plague upon the land.

A thoroughgoing amelioration of these conditions was attempted by the statute of 1601 of Queen Elizabeth,[11] which brought about a thorough regulation by law of the system of helping and supporting the poor. This statute divided the paupers into those who could not work and those who were too lazy to work. The former were to

[10] By the above-mentioned law (see note 7), specified groups of persons were compelled to perform agricultural labor. The farmers therefore had no occasion to attract labor by offering higher wages.

[11] *An Act for the Relief of the Poor,* 43 Eliz. c. 2 (probably worked out by Francis Bacon), the foundation of the English poor law until 1834; see Nicholls, *op. cit.,* i, 194.

be cared for in almshouses (where provision was also made for taking poor children for the purpose of educating them to work); the latter were to be compelled to perform certain labor, at an officially fixed wage, instead of being whipped, as before, and then dismissed with no means of support.[12] To cover the costs of this plan, and in place of the contributions which had hitherto been more or less voluntary, the law introduced compulsory contributions, which took the form of a tax allotted to each parish, the richer parishes being required to help bear the burdens of poor parishes.

The various measures undertaken by the government for preventing the concentration of the poor in cities, especially London,[13] and for finding the means of securing more general prosperity, as well as the numerous proposals of private persons, offer proof of the degree to which poverty was gaining the upper hand. In accordance with the mercantile point of view, it was recommended, as a means of raising the level of prosperity, that industries be developed which contributed to the export

[12] The good effects of this law were partly nullified by the law of 1662 (13 & 14 Car. II, c. 12), which practically bound many laborers to the soil, and made it impossible for them to seek the best opportunities for work. The growth in the number of unemployed, brought about by this law, led to the establishment of workhouses; see Nicholls, *op. cit.,* i, 293ff.

[13] In this connection the strange edicts should be mentioned whereby repeated attempts were made between 1580 and 1674 to prevent the increase in the population of London. The building of new houses was forbidden, and unoccupied houses were torn down; the country nobles were forbidden to maintain a steady residence in the capital, because too much money was withdrawn from the rural communities; and on certain days fasting was ordained for the benefit of the poor. See Sir Frederic Morton Eden, *The State of the Poor, or a History of the Labouring Classes in England . . .,* 3 vols., London 1797; see also David Macpherson, *Annals of Commerce, Manufactures,* etc., London 1805, ii, 289, 364, 373.

trade. Work by women and children did actually become established later on a very large scale, with the introduction of the practice of division of labor; but, contrary to expectation, the misery of the poor continually increased.

For the mechanization of the processes of labor made employers more and more independent of the individual skill of their employees, and thus the reason for treating them with any special consideration disappeared. The protection afforded by the laws failed in connection with newly rising industries,[14] and the workers were utterly unable to defend their interests themselves because of the strict laws against organizing.[15] According to the general view of economic historians they were more isolated, and more impotent, during the seventeenth century than ever before or after. A combination of unfortunate circumstances kept them permanently in straits. It is probably safe to assume that the taxes, and, after the outbreak of the Civil War, the burden of quartered soldiers, aggravated by the rising cost of living, had been shifted so as to fall upon that stratum of the population which was least able to bear them; but in addition to this, a series of unusually severe famine years contributed toward making the situation worse.[16] Prices of meat rose 50 per cent,[17] the prices of bread 100 per cent. Wages, on the

[14] During the seventeenth century cloth manufacturing and the iron industry took on special importance. After the revocation of the Edict of Nantes (1685) numerous skilled craftsmen of France emigrated to England, and silk spinning and cotton printing showed marked increase.

[15] See Hewins, *op. cit.,* p. 112.

[16] The famine years were 1646-51 and 1658-61; the worst year of all was 1661.

[17] The inadequate transportation facilities accentuated the distress. According to Macaulay (Thomas B. Macaulay, *The History of England* . . ., Boston 1856, i, 292), the markets were often inaccessible through

55

contrary, remained stationary. And in this time of the greatest distress, religion and politics absorbed the public interest so completely that the terrible condition of the lower classes attracted little attention.[18] Rogers truly says: "The seventeenth century fastened pauperism on the English labourer, and this is his only inheritance in the strife of that time." [19]

This brief statement may serve as a general characterization of the economic status of England during the first half of the seventeenth century. These were the conditions with which the Quakers had to contend when, in the course of their efforts to mitigate the direst need, they began to lay the foundations among their adherents for their doctrine of the universal priesthood of believers.

The ultimate aim of the first great Quakers was to ameliorate poverty over the whole country, by securing the combined action of the various sects in helping the poor. Through this activity they hoped to bring about a lessening of the existing religious differences—after they had come to realize that it was unlikely that all England would be convinced of their doctrine. Abolition of begging, the erection of almshouses, and a general regulation of the whole system of caring for the poor, which in spite

---

several months of the year, owing to the condition of the roads, so that crops were often allowed to rot in the fields in one location, while in another only a few miles away the supply was not nearly sufficient to meet the demand. Until 1663 the traffic in grain between different parts of the country was further restricted by law.

[18] This in spite of occasional demonstrations, as for instance those made by women in the court of the Parliament building in Feb. 1642 and August 1643. See S. R. Gardiner, *Fall of the Monarchy of Charles I*, ii, 421, and *History of the Great Civil War*, London 1886-91, i, 218.

[19] Rogers, *op. cit.*, p. 266.

of the laws was in very bad shape, seemed difficult but not impossible. "Our lovingkindness should be as all-embracing as the love of God; and if we add to it faith and industry, mountains of difficulty will disappear like mists before the sun" (Bellers). The Quakers recognized the amelioration of the situation of the lower classes as the most pressing duty not only of all individuals but also, in particular, of the government, and referred to this duty in many petitions and pamphlets.[20] "Let all the poor, the blind, the lame, and the crippled be cared for, so that no beggar may be found on English soil, and so that you can claim to be the equals of the Jews; for they had the Law, which provided for widows, orphans, and strangers. Whoever closes his ear to the poor, closes it to the Law."

And the means for doing this? First, systematic organization of charity instead of unregulated almsgiving; and secondly, a leveling off of the social inequalities —for the crushing distress of the lower classes stood in sharp contrast to the senseless luxury of the upper strata of society.[21] The sense of a duty to society must be awakened in the latter; but a quicker way would be the prohibition of all frivolous amusement and of unreasonable

[20] For instance, George Fox, *To the Protector and Parliament of England,* London 1658, and *To the Parliament of the Commonwealth of England,* London 1659; also Thomas Lawson, *An Appeal to the Parliament, concerning the Poor, that there may not be a Beggar in England,* London 1660.

[21] See S. R. Gardiner, *History of the Great Civil War,* iii, 4ff., and Wolfgang Michael, *Cromwell,* ii, 27. A report of Johann Friedrich Schlezer, the minister from Brandenburg at the court of Cromwell, runs: "A pound is thought of as lightly here as a reichsthaler (about three shillings) among us."

extravagance in clothing. "Clothe the naked and feed the hungry from what is left over." [22]

It was to be expected, in view of the unsettled condition of society, that such agitation, zeal and devotion, would have but little influence where influence would count. The government went on its way after the Restoration as before, and left to private organizations the task of working out their ideals in practice, though their ability to do so often lagged far behind their desire.

Very little has been published regarding the humanitarian activity of the Quakers within their own membership, although the fact that there were no Quakers among those supported at public expense was referred to by Eden as being especially noteworthy, [23] and the means by which this situation had been brought about was held up for imitation. He writes: "The time may come when a wise legislator may descend to inquire, by what medium a whole society, in both the old and new world, is made to think and act with uniformity for upwards of a century;—by what polity, without emolument from Government, they have become the only people on earth free from poverty;—by what economy they have thus prevented beggary and want among any of their members, whilst the nation groans under taxes for the poor." [24] The Society itself has given no information as to the kind and extent of its care for the needy. There seems to have

[22] Disapproval of extravagance is often expressed by Fox and Penn in pamphlets directed to individual groups according to their vocation; also in Penn's *No Cross, No Crown,* and in *Some Fruits of Solitude in Reflections and Maxims.*

[23] Eden, *op. cit.,* i, 588, 589.

[24] Eden here quotes from Dr. J. C. Lettsom, *Memoirs of John Fothergill, M.D.,* London 1786. See Eden, *op. cit.,* i, 588.

been no interest at all in collecting records for following generations. Whereas all religious persecutions of Quakers are carefully recorded,[25] references to their social work are only to be found scattered through letters, pamphlets, and diaries, and in the minute books. These latter, to be sure, in so far as they concern the central organization for all England, are still extant and almost complete in the principal office of the Society in London; but there are now numerous subordinate meetings located in various parts of England, and the division of territory has changed in many ways in the course of 260 years, so that a search through their minutes offers difficulties which are out of all proportion to the possible yield. Moreover, it is now impossible to secure evidence as to the size and constitution of the Society at that time.[26] An exhaustive presentation of the facts is therefore out of the question; and in the following observations we can give only a general view, discussing a few of the measures which derive their especial significance mainly from the time in which they were evolved.

For this purpose it appears necessary to explain more fully the organization of the Society, briefly touched upon in the Introduction. The division into monthly and quarterly meetings, and Yearly Meeting, which exists down to the present, cannot be said to have been worked

[25] Joseph Besse's work, *A Collection of the Sufferings* . . ., was compiled on the basis of the reports made in all the monthly meetings, which were forwarded each year to the Yearly Meeting.

[26] The first detailed statistics on the number of members and regular attenders, and on the total number of meetings for worship held, were forwarded to the Yearly Meeting of 1862. All earlier statements are based upon estimates, and are considered to be unreliable, in part, even by the Quakers.

out in practice before [27] 1668. And yet we find in ancient records [28] that even as early as 1653 there were monthly meetings in Durham, Swarthmore, and a few other places not specifically named, in which there was a demand for meetings "to effect reimbursal for the great sums that have been paid out." According to George Fox, [29] the wish soon arose for a wider extension of these periodic meetings for transacting business: "In 1653, in Cumberland, many of the Elders came to me at Swarthmore, in Lancashire, and desired that they might have a Monthly Meeting, to look after the poor, and to see that all walked according to the Truth, etc.; and they had a meeting settled there for the same purpose. . . .

"And then there was a Yearly Meeting settled at Skipton in Yorkshire, for all the northern and southern counties [presumably in 1657] [30] . . .

"And after[wards] the Yearly Meeting was kept at Balby in Yorkshire, where there were many thousands of people: and likewise at Skipton the same year, by the Elders there ordered from all parts, in the year 1660. And from thence, it was removed to London the next year, where it hath been kept ever since, as being looked upon a more convenient place. And there we had intelligence from all parts beyond the seas, how the Truth prospered and spread in both England, Wales, Ireland, Scotland, America, Holland, and Germany . . . and all the

[27] *Yearly Meeting Epistles,* vol. i, p. vii.
[28] See A. R. Barclay, *Letters, etc., of Early Friends,* vol. vii of *A Select Series, Biographical, Narrative, Epistolary, and Miscellaneous, . . .,* of which vols. i-v were edited by John Barclay, new edition London 1835-45.
[29] A. R. Barclay, *op. cit.,* pp. 312-314.
[30] See W. C. Braithwaite, *The Beginnings of Quakerism,* p. 332.

sufferings were brought or sent up hither [viz., to the Yearly Meeting] from all parts of the world where Friends were. . . . And there was not any public collection, but what was done at the Yearly Meeting (with the consent of all Friends from all parts), for all general purposes."

In this document we have in broad outlines the plan and purpose of the monthly meetings and Yearly Meeting.[31] The care of the poor and maintenance of the discipline were the special concerns of the monthly meetings, but the care of those who had been persecuted for their faith's sake was considered to be the concern of the Society as a whole, as were its relations with Quakers in foreign countries, and the other general affairs of the Yearly Meeting. The quarterly meeting, which was introduced between the Yearly Meeting and the monthly meetings in the later fifties of the seventeenth century,[32] served to simplify the business of the Yearly Meeting, and made quicker action possible upon a multitude of matters which were outside the jurisdiction of the monthly meeting, and which without the quarterly meeting could have been attended to but once a year. Yet it is impossible to determine accurately the scope of the activities of the quarterly meeting for the first decades, as the earliest minute books that have been preserved date from 1690. Since the quarterly

[31] The functions of the different meetings are more explicitly defined in the Epistle of the meeting in Durham of 1659. See *Yearly Meeting Epistles,* vol. 1, pp. xxxi-xxxiv.

[32] According to the *Journal,* however (ii, 80), the quarterly meetings came into existence before the monthly meetings. They apparently had the functions of the later monthly meetings, but were held only once in three months. London Yearly Meeting was established in 1660.

meetings, moreover, are less involved in the humanitarian activities of the Quakers, we shall devote our attention primarily to the monthly meetings.

In view of the uniform organization of these meetings —they all received the same instructions from the central authority (that is, the Yearly Meeting), and were expected to return written reports to it, which were summarized in the Yearly Meeting minutes—it appears permissible to speak of the relief measures adopted by all of the monthly meetings on the evidence of the minutes of the Yearly Meeting and the minutes of the few monthly meetings whose records are accessible. Within the narrow limits of such a monthly meeting it was possible to revive the character of the primitive Christian community.[33] The elders and overseers had, as it were, the functions of parents or teachers; but this did not lead to any personal domination nor tend to weaken the obligation of other members to mutual helpfulness and support.

It was taken as a self-evident principle that everyone should endeavor to support himself through his own work.[34] An indirect inducement to do so was certainly afforded, especially for the more sensitive natures, by the fact that the circumstances of all those who had asked the monthly meeting for help were publicly discussed in the monthly meeting, in the presence of all the members. Only in cases having to do with the support of the depend-

[33] That this was the ultimate goal of Quaker effort may be seen from Penn's *Primitive Christianity Revived,* London 1696, and from other evidence.

[34] A strengthening of the sense of personal responsibility was especially necessary at that period throughout the nation, because of the frequent cases in which the man of the family deserted.

ents of traveling preachers was publicity avoided: the fact that the activity of the breadwinner was for the common good removed the odium from his need of public support.[35]

Any person in need of help could apply to the meeting personally, or through some other member. But in order that persons who needed help, but were too timid or proud to say so, should not suffer actual want, the elders and overseers or, sometimes, visiting committees specially appointed for the purpose, had the duty of watching continuously over the circumstances of all the members, and of reporting cases which in their judgment needed help to the next monthly meeting. In urgent cases, as numerous examples show, they did what was needed themselves, expecting that their outlay would be made good by the meeting. If it appeared that support would be needed over a considerable period of time, as when a member was unable to work, a thorough investigation was made of the actual need, and the most appropriate kind of care was considered. An attempt was first made to secure the coöperation of members of the family, for whom remunerative work was secured in order to make it possible for them to contribute. Not until this plan proved impracticable did the meeting step in.

It was usual for the meeting to assure itself that the expense could be met of certain primary requirements, as a dwelling and sufficient fuel. The latter probably received special consideration because coal had greatly

[35] This point, among others, is emphasized in *Sundry Ancient Epistles,* xxvi, 3 (1699).

risen in price,[36] like many of the means of subsistence, after the passage of the Navigation Acts. Attempts were made to mitigate the price by ordering in large quantities. Thus there appears more or less regularly, every few months, the entry: "The account for coals for the poor was balanced." A dwelling was provided either by paying the rent directly or by arranging for the admission of the needy person—and this method was adopted presumably only for persons without any family connections—in so-called charity rooms; in such cases a sensible effort was made, whenever possible, to put two persons together who, though they might be helpless when separate, could complement each other and thus avoid the necessity of further support.

In addition to care of this sort, there seems to have been a certain amount of care of sick persons without means, within their own families: the account books list expenditures for medicines, and show that free burial in the graveyards of the Friends was given to destitute persons who died. We may note here that an effort was made to inter destitute persons, as well as those who were better off, with simplicity, yet with due dignity; so that active participation in the funerals of the poor was considered a duty of members.

In concluding our discussion of the provision of necessities, we may refer to the fact that in the first years of the existence of the Quaker meetings it was sometimes customary, following business meetings, to make a distri-

[36] Coal, because of the high transportation costs, could be brought to its destination only by water, and in the south of England the term "sea coal" was therefore used; see Macaulay, *op. cit.*, i, 294.

bution of bread to the needy, in accordance with the examples cited in the Bible.[37] Yet the expenditure for such distributions was always much less than the total that was officially granted to the needy at each business meeting, whether or not the required amount was realized in the collection held at the same time; for it usually happened that individual members were able and willing to advance the necessary moneys. The meeting in such cases expressly pledged itself to reimbursal.

Support of a needy person was generally handed over to a caretaker, who gave assistance in installments, according to his judgment. The minutes name the caretaker as well as the person receiving help, and there is evidence in the records that in some cases persons were supported who were not members of the Society. Quakers are mostly called "poor Friends"; but there are entries in the form: "Paid to John Haddon for Edward Hall, a person in need, and the widow Cane, a poor old woman, 16 s.," or "Paid to J. Hill for the widow Massey, who is sick and almost blind, 5 s."; and such entries indicate that the persons helped were not members of the Society. It should be remarked, however, that membership in a meeting was not very well regulated until 1737;[38] after this year the designation "member" came into official use, and at the same time admission was made easier through the introduction of so-called "birthright membership." Down

[37] Fox's *Journal* (manuscript): "And many times there woulde bee two hundred beggars of ye worlde (there for all ye country knewe wee mett about ye poore) which after ye meetinge was donne, freinds woulde sende to ye bakers & give ym each a loafe a peice bee ym as many as woulde." See the Cambridge *Journal*, i, 356.

[38] Yearly Meeting Minutes for 1737.

to this time it had been the custom not to consider any one a "Friend" unless he was ready to bear testimony as martyr to his faith.

In consideration of the varying constitution of individual meetings, and in accordance with the principle observed in the public care of the poor, it was considered necessary for the wealthier meetings to help bear the burdens of the poorer ones.[39] This plan was carried out by means of a central agency in London, the Six Weeks' Meeting, through its subcommittee, the Meeting of Twelve, which reviewed all the financial affairs of the Society and which also paid the Society's contribution to the parish poor fund; for the Quakers were by no means excused from making their proportional contribution toward the public support of paupers.

The Quakers soon began to make an effort to collect special funds for the purpose of supporting the poor, and to urge their richer members to make legacies and gifts to this end. The result of this effort is shown in the Trust Property Books. It is clear from these books that capital sums which are still producing an income in the twentieth century came into the possession of the Society as early as 1665, 1670, 1672, 1683, etc. Such gifts were occasionally made with the proviso that a stated annuity was to be paid to the donor during his life—a practice which during the first unsettled years must certainly have been an inducement to members to bequeath their property to the meeting.

[39] In the course of time the policy came to be adopted of assessing each meeting a specific sum, according to its ability to pay, for charitable purposes.

We see further from the account books of the monthly meetings that sums were repeatedly paid out for immediate distribution to specified groups of needy persons or to the poor in general. It is to be presumed, however, that, in view of the great need, all these measures were not enough to carry out Fox's injunction that there should not be a single beggar in England. Wars and extraordinary visitations, such as the devastations of the plague in 1665 and the burning to ashes of a considerable part of the capital in 1666, disturbed the course of economic life.[40] At the same time the savage persecution of dissenters made increased demands upon the liberality of the Quaker congregations. Special meetings were therefore appointed, which dealt exclusively with the question of the care of the poor—and even this fact did not shield them always from being forcibly broken up by the authorities.[41]

We have somewhat more information about an organization of women members, which Fox himself called into being probably about 1658. During his visits to the various meetings he had recognized the necessity of securing the help of the women, and with the assistance of a certain Sara Blackbourne (or Blackbury) he succeeded in assembling a circle of sixty women, who watched over the

[40] Gregory King (1648-1712), a British genealogist, engraver, and statistician, estimates that the number of paupers in need of support at this time comprised one fifth of the total population. Under Charles II the poor rates amounted to far more than the yield of the excise tax and the customs, namely, to £700,000—nearly half of the total income of the crown. Macaulay, *op. cit.*, i, 223, 224.

[41] This may be assumed from cases cited in Besse's *Sufferings,* vol. i. On the other hand, Fox's *Journal* (manuscript) states that these efforts of the Quakers were acknowledged with approval and their continuance recommended. See the Cambridge *Journal,* i, 356.

interests of the poor and sick, of widows and orphans, and above all of their fellow members who were in jail. At that time no public provision was made for feeding prisoners, or at least totally insufficient provision; but a well organized service of the Friends attempted in spite of all difficulties to meet the most pressing material needs.[42] The first organization of women joined later with the Box Meeting, which was established at about the same time and still exists—called by this name because a shilling was deposited in a box at the beginning of each session by each woman present. In addition to these contributions special funds made extensive charity work possible, and it often happened that needy individuals were referred by the monthly meeting to the care of the Box Meeting. Information regarding the extent of these charitable activities is to be found in certain "Epistles" from the women Friends in London regarding the work and purpose of the women's meetings,[43] from which it can be seen that there were similar organizations outside of London, or that, at least, in these outside meetings the women, who constituted on the average a third of the membership,[44] engaged in similar work.

The meetings by no means limited their activities to the

[42] See *The History of the Life of Thomas Ellwood, written by himself* (originally published London 1714), new edition by S. Graveson, London 1906, pp. 132, 133, 195. The conditions in English prisons are discussed in detail in Chapter V, p. 162ff., of the present volume.

[43] For example, the *Epistle from Women Friends of London about the service and ends of Women's Meetings, for Women Friends in the Counties and elsewhere,* January 4, 1674. For the origin of the name "Box Meeting," see Beck and Ball, p. 349.

[44] Commendation and defense of such work by women is also to be found in Fox's epistles; for instance: *This is an Encouragement to all the Women's Meetings in the World,* 1676.

care of the poor who had been compelled to accept doles as a result of age and sickness—Quakerism had repudiated absolutely the theory that the poor should be used as a ladder to heaven—; [45] but very vigorous efforts were made to prevent the increase of pauperism, as well as to help those who had become impoverished, so that they might rise again to a condition of independent self-support. For this purpose the feeling of the close relationship of all the members with one another proved to be both necessary and effective. Only through exact knowledge of their financial circumstances was it possible convincingly to dissuade those who had no property from undertakings which seemed likely to endanger their economic status.

In general an effort was made to discourage any emigration which did not appear to have compelling reasons in its favor, or indeed any change of residence which was hastily entered upon or which gave but little promise of improvement. [46] In any case the meeting was to be notified of an intention to move, and, if persons were involved

[45] A vivid picture of this Catholic custom is given in the introduction to Paul Sabatier's *Vie de S. François d'Assise* (Life of Saint Francis of Assisi), 9th edition Paris 1894, p. xiii. Even in England the idea of the necessity of having the poor was retained by many persons far into the eighteenth century. Sir Matthew Hale, in *A Discourse touching Provision for the Poor* (in *The Works, Moral and Religious, of Sir Matthew Hale, Knt.*, London 1805, i, 516), still retains the Catholic point of view: "A due care for the provision of the poor is an act, 1, of great piety toward Almighty God. . . . It is one of those great tributes that he justly requires from the rest of mankind; which, because they cannot pay to him, he hath scattered the poor amongst the rest of mankind as his substitutes and receivers." And Bernard de Mandeville, in *Fable of the Bees*, 1723, says: "It would be easier to live without money than to live without the poor." Without hunger as a stimulus to exertion industrial development appears to him to be unthinkable.

[46] See, for instance, Yearly Meeting Epistles for 1679, 1693, etc.

who were not in comfortable circumstances, the justification for moving and the possibility of getting employment in the prospective place of residence were carefully examined, and any possible undesirable labor competition was considered which might result from the move, to the disadvantage of Friends already living there. Only when the outcome appeared certain was such a person granted official permission to move; for in case he or his dependents became destitute, the meeting last attended had the duty of support over a period of several years. Such support was voluntary rather than mandatory during the early years; but it was definitely and officially declared to be an obligation in 1710,[47] after the London meetings, in particular, had attempted to protect themselves against being overwhelmed by the burden of supporting newcomers, and had requested contributions for this purpose from the home meetings.

The Quakers who left England for the sake of their faith, or persons who emigrated for other reasons, could rely upon support in case of need, through either outright gifts or loans at a low rate of interest (mostly two per

[47] The Law of Settlement of 1710, with amendments of 1711 and 1737, confirmed by statute the claim of a person to be supported or assisted by the meeting near his place of residence after he had resided there for three years. If a person had previously been in need of support, the meeting granted him immediate help, but called upon the meeting of his previous residence for reimbursal. Full membership, and hence the right to support, might be acquired in less than three years by the following classes of persons: 1, all persons who had already assisted either by gifts of money or by services rendered, in bearing the burdens of the meeting; 2, domestic servants, after one year of faithful service; 3, apprentices, after forty days' work with their masters. With respect to the right of support, the residence of the husband counted as the residence of his wife and children, irrespective of the length of their stay in the district of the meeting in question; also, after the death of the husband, the claims of the wife and children remained unaffected.

cent). Such loans were also liberally made to those who wished to set themselves up in business at home, especially at the close of their apprenticeship, if the meeting considered them worthy of help. Some meetings possessed dowry funds, from which the poorer persons of both sexes received sums of money (mostly £40) which made it possible for them to begin housekeeping in a suitable way.

We may mention one more special source of help, which in many cases amounted to prevention of destitution, namely the funds, raised by popular subscription, for those whose houses had been burned down. A fund of this kind was raised after every fire, even when the victim made no special request for help. To be sure, the only point about this practice that was peculiar to the Quakers was the fact that contributions were voluntary; for such collections were in accordance with a practice that persisted in England into the nineteenth century. Fire insurance did not come into use until 1749, and made its way very slowly; for the so-called fire brief, or royal authorization to levy taxes within specified districts for the benefit of those who had been burned out, provided indemnification of loss, the more dependable as the governmental officials [8] were accustomed to collect the contributions with especial zeal.

There is evidence that the Quakers were sometimes negligent in contributing to these collections, and were taken to task because of this negligence. It is no wonder, however, that they were somewhat remiss; for they were

---

[8] The Secretary of Briefs to the Lord Chancellor sent copies of the fire briefs to all persons in the district in question who were under obligation to contribute. Fire briefs were abolished by law in 1828.

obliged to contribute to the public poor fund, though they never appealed to public funds for their own members, and in addition had to submit every year to extensive confiscation of their property because of their refusal to pay the church tithes. The amounts involved in their losses can be seen in the financial records of the Meeting for Sufferings, a standing committee which was established in 1675 primarily for the indemnification of those who had been taxed by the authority of the fire briefs, and which has attended to this task for over 200 years, expending in 1857, for instance, over £6000 for such indemnities, though by then the scale of punishment had been mitigated and the number of members considerably diminished.[49]

The cases of persons who, though able to work, fell into a condition of need in spite of all these preventive measures offered the Quakers their first real problem in the theory and practice of social work. They were not satisfied, as recorded above, with mere temporary amelioration, but sought to enable the poor to work their way up through their own powers; they afforded *help toward self-help*. Such a purpose, though it can often be carried out at less money expense than other measures of relief, requires increased expenditure of personal attention on the part of the caretaker, because of the necessity of the strictly individualized character of the care. The minutes of the meetings report cases in which all that was considered necessary was guidance in the orderly management of home affairs or in improved business methods, in order to enable a family to get along with its available

[49] Yearly Meeting Minutes for 1857—the first year in which the minutes were printed. Abolition of the church tithes followed in 1868.

POOR RELIEF

resources. How far such efforts were crowned with success, however, or how often, when they produced no
results, the member involved was expelled from the
Society, cannot be ascertained.

If the needy person knew no trade at all to which he
was fitted, an effort was made to find some sort of work
that he could do—a measure which proved effective in
discouraging those who were unwilling to work, and who
might otherwise abuse the liberality of the Quakers, from
joining the Society. To a certain extent the difficulty of
finding work within the Society was increased by the principles of the Quakers; for they frowned upon luxury in
those days rather more than now, even for the well-to-do.
There was therefore but little occupation for artisans,
except in so far as they manufactured objects absolutely
necessary to life. The maintenance of large retinues of
servants was, and still is, taboo, because of the unproduc-
tiveness of their work; it was thought that their powers
could be made more serviceable to the community in some
other way. An attempt was made to find employment
under Quaker masters for members who were of the
servant class, on the assumption that they were only sat-
isfying a need for domestic servants which they considered justifiable; almost every monthly meeting procured a
few such situations for its members. The matter was
generally accomplished very simply. For instance, if
"Friend A" was seeking a position as helper or "Friend
"B" a position as maidservant, "Friend C" or "Friend D"
made known a willingness to take the applicant, and the
person so hired could not leave his position without the
consent of the meeting.

Naturally, not all the employment needs were satisfied in this way, and so the quarterly meetings had the task of lending assistance to their members in obtaining positions within their larger jurisdictions. They maintained lists [50] in which entries occur from 1694 on. The care of unemployed maidservants was the special concern of the women's meetings. Even when domestic servants entered the employ of non-Quakers they remained under the care of a meeting, which gave them the feeling of having something to fall back upon in case of need.[51]

In addition to the above, we should mention a central bureau for bringing together prospective employers and employees, the establishment of which was planned in London when the activity of the meetings had proved to be insufficient to meet the needs. This plan, to be sure, does not come to the fore until 1805, and was not put into effect until several years later. The activity of the new organization, if we may judge from reports, was of very modest scope; yet at that the Quakers were very far ahead of their time. The idea of establishing this bureau was like that of most of the undertakings of the Quakers, in that it was due in its essentials to the very earliest Quakers.[52] George Fox had advocated the setting up of official employment bureaus in every market!

Along with domestic servants and employees of all kinds there were always persons present in the earlier

[50] Beck and Ball, p. 72.

[51] Penn had also a provision, in Article xxiii of his outline of the constitution for Pennsylvania, 1682 (see *Minutes of the Provincial Council of Pennsylvania*, Philadelphia 1852, i, 39), that lists should be maintained for all domestic servants, in which the names of the parties, time of service, wages, and pay days should be designated.

[52] For instance, see Lawson, *op. cit.*, p. 2.

Quaker communities who were more or less able to work, and for whom some home work had to be procured to enable them to eke out a living. In the *Letters, etc., of Early Friends* (vol. vii of Barclay's *Select Series,* etc.), we find as early as 1662 the record of the determination to give such persons employment; in 1676 the minutes report that spinning is considered appropriate work for poor Friends, and the Meeting of Twelve is commissioned to expend £100 for flax. In each monthly meeting one member is to be appointed whose duty it is to distribute the raw material to the spinners, to pay them for their work, and to deliver the yarn to weavers. Further directions for the oversight of home work follow in 1679, after the Society had officially adopted the rule, in accordance with what had long been the actual practice, that no appeal should be made to public funds for the support of their poor.

The documents, however, give us little information as to whether there were any disrupting economic consequences of establishing a home industry of this kind, nor are we told how the products were marketed. Indeed, the movement is of interest to us only indirectly, as representing the preliminary stage of the policy of institutional care of the poor in workhouses, which the Society established about the turn of the century. This policy was developed from the reform plans of the humanitarian John Bellers,[53] one of the most distinguished of the early

[53] John Bellers (1654-1725), born of a well-to-do family, the friend of William Penn, unable to pursue a political career because of his Quakerism, devoted himself to various studies and philanthropic undertakings; see *Dictionary of National Biography.* A detailed account of Bellers's activity is found in Eduard Bernstein, *Cromwell and Communism,* London

Quakers, and had been given to the public years before, in part, by George Fox and Thomas Lawson, in the form of addresses to Parliament. Bellers's best known work is entitled *Proposals for raising a Colledge of Industry*,[54] the ideas of which, with variations and additions, recur in his other writings. Their originality justifies a careful examination.

Bellers aims at three objectives with these workers' colonies: "First, profit for the rich (which will be life to the rest). Secondly, a plentiful living for the poor, without difficulty. Thirdly, a good education for youth, that may tend to prepare their souls into the nature of good ground."[55] The first point, which was the occasion of wonder, is explained as follows: "However prevalent arguments of charity may be to some, when profit is joyned with it, it will raise most money, provide for most people, hold longest, and do most good: for what sap is to a tree, that profit is to all business, by increasing and keeping it alive."[56]

Bellers explains his plans with a practical example. He assumes that a capital sum of £18,000 has been raised, in shares of a par value of £25, to be used as follows:

1930 (translated by H. J. Stenning from *Sozialismus und Demokratie in der grossen englischen Revolution* (Socialism and democracy in the great English revolution), 4th edition Stuttgart 1922), p. 253ff. All the statements in the present work, however, rest upon first-hand sudy of Bellers's original writings.

[54] *Proposals for raising a Colledge of Industry of all useful Trades and Husbandry, with Profit for the Rich, a Plentiful Living for the Poor, and a Good Education for the Youth,* printed by T. Sowle 1696. A direct occasion for publishing this work was afforded by the disturbances among the weavers as a result of the introduction of cotton and other cloths from India, which deprived many English workmen of their bread.

[55] Bellers, *op. cit.*, p. 1.

[56] Bellers, *op. cit.*, p. 2.

£10,000 for the purchase of land.

2,000 for the purchase of equipment, cattle, seed corn, etc.

3,000 for all that may be needed to enable craftsmen of various kinds to ply their trade.

3,000 for new buildings or the repair of old ones.

On this tract there shall be settled 300 persons [57] whose distribution among the various callings (farmers, artisans of all kinds, and laborers) is specifically prescribed; and Bellers calculates that 200 are sufficient to support the colony, so that the remaining 100 can work for the profit of those who advance the capital.[58] If the annual value of the work of each person is put at only £10, there results a net profit of about 5½ per cent; if at £15, the net profit is about 8½ per cent.[59] This seems well within reach, but even if the earnings do not come up to expectations, the undertaking remains profitable; for the savings to be effected through efficient organization must be taken into account. The plan of providing a central dwelling and a central table prevents the wastefulness of small-scale housekeeping. All clothing that is manufactured is put to use in some way, whereas in ordinary busi-

[57] In later editions Bellers increases the amount of capital and the number of inhabitants required for such a colony.

[58] As to the way in which they shall be employed, however, nothing specific is said; except that for colonies that are established on the seacoast Bellers recommends fishing, for which an outside market is available.

[59] In his *Essays about the Poor, Manufactures, Trade, Plantation, and Immorality,* London 1699, which appeared three years later, Bellers assumes that every worker is able to support himself and one other person, and thus that a full half of the colony would be able to work for the profit of the enterprise, and that each one would produce goods worth £20 annually, yielding nearly 17% profit.

ness many articles lose their market value because of slight faults that in no way interfere with their usefulness. All the costs of merchandising disappear. Agriculture can be carried on in the most rational way; in order that the crops may be harvested more quickly, artisans are to be called in at harvest time to help—a plan which is in the interest of their own health besides. From the cultivation of the northern regions, which are largely fallow and sparsely populated, very great advantage would accrue to agriculture as a whole, and the property of the great landowners would appreciate in value.

There are also numerous advantages for members of such colonies who are without property (for the colonies are thought of as being intended exclusively for persons who cannot support themselves). The initial difficulty of accustoming the older people to a communal life in "colleges" will naturally disappear in the course of time; in fourteen or fifteen years a young generation may grow up which is completely adapted to this life. Money will be abolished, and with it one of the principal causes of dissension. "This colledge-fellowship will make labour, and not money, the standard to value all necessaries by; and tho' money hath its conveniences, in the common way of living, it being a pledge among men for want of credit; yet not without its mischiefs; and [is] call'd by our Saviour, *The Mammon of Unrighteousness;* most cheats and robberies would go but slowly on, if it were not for money. . . . Money in the body politick, is what a crutch is to the natural body, cripled; but when the body is sound, the crutch is but troublesome: so when the particular interest is made a publick interest, in such a colledge money will be of little use there." [60]

With the abolition of the principle of competition the cause of much distress and unnecessarily hard labor disappears. People who previously were poor and miserable are provided, as colonists, with the necessities of life in their well days and their sick days; "and if parents die their children [will be] well educated, and preserved from misery, and their marrying encouraged, which is now generally discouraged." [61] This brings Bellers [62] to the point which of itself seems to him sufficient to decide the argument in favor of the establishment of such colonies—their value as places of education for the young.[63] In another place Bellers says: [64] "The poor have very ill qualities, and are as ill tutors, as well as evil examples to their children, and therefore it's of absolute necessity their children should have better instructors, and a more industrious education than their parents will give them; the happiness of the next age much depending upon the good education of the children of this." In a workers' colony the children can be instructed in all useful knowledge, and

[60] Bellers, *Proposals,* pp. 3, 4.

[61] Bellers, *op. cit.,* pp. 12, 13.

[62] Bellers is probably thinking here principally of the Settlement Act of 1662 (13 & 14 Car. II. c. 12), by the terms of which the right of settlement (that is, the establishment of legal residence, with the right to public support if indigent) was more difficult for married laborers to secure than for unmarried laborers. There resulted an increase in the number of illegitimate children, who automatically acquired residence, so far as their claim to public support was concerned, in their birthplace or in the legal residence of their mothers.

[63] The steps taken by Quakers toward the education of children is discussed in a special chapter (Chapter II) of the present work; but we mention the matter here in order not to interrupt the continuity.

[64] Bellers, *Essays about the Poor, Manufactures,* . . ., p. 3.

79

in their free time they can see others work and thus learn a trade, "work being no more labour than play." No elaborate preparation is made for hours of formal instruction: "Men will grow strong with working, but not with thinking." [65] In any event, nobody shall be compelled to study by means of corporal punishment. "Beyond reading and writing, a multitude of scholars is not so useful to the publick as some think; the body requiring more hands and legs to provide for, and support it, than heads to direct it; and if the head grows too big for the body, the whole will fall into the rickets." [66]

According to Bellers's view, children of both sexes could be taught reading as well as knitting and spinning in four or five years, and the larger boys could be taught turning, "and beginning young, they would make the best artists." [67]

To sum up, all the advantages which Bellers enumerates amount to this, that the poor who are now out of employment could work at producing the means of living, and other articles manufactured in industry, which would be as valuable to England as the mines to Spain. "The poor who are out of employment are like diamonds in the rough; their value is not appreciated. A people engaged in steady work, on the contrary, is the greatest treasure of the Kingdom; without laborers there are no lords, for if the poor laborers did not produce much more means of nourishment and articles of commerce than they consumed

[65] Bellers, *Proposals,* p. 16.
[66] Bellers, *op. cit.,* p. 17.
[67] Bellers, *op. cit.,* p. 17.

in their own use, every lord would have to *become* a laborer also, or all idle persons would starve. But the polishing of these diamonds, that their lustre and value may appear, is a subject worth the consideration and endeavor of our greatest statesmen and senators." [68] Supplying such persons with work would not only take care of the normal population of the poor, but would bring back many discharged soldiers, and also induce many thousands of immigrants from foreign lands, and "the more people we get from foreign lands, the more we attract their power to ourselves."

At the conclusion of one of the later editions of his *Proposals,* Bellers answers numerous objections; but in these answers he overlooks, perhaps intentionally, the very real danger that there would be no market for the products of the labor of that part of the colony which works to create the entrepreneur's profit. When Bellers refers to the fact that in bad times the poor are always able to exist more cheaply in communities than alone, he assumes, by implication, that those engaged in the enterprise would not be able to withdraw their capital under such conditions, though as a matter of fact, it is probable that a different utilization of the land, buildings, etc., would be possible, or that at least the raw material might

[68] By neglecting the matter of the regular employment of the poor, English economic life suffered a loss, according to Bellers's estimate, of £3,900,000 a year; for of the seven million who belonged to the nation, five hundred thousand are unemployed, and these could earn on an average sixpence a day; whereas under current conditions they receive public support as paupers which, if the cost is reckoned at only a shilling a week per capita, amounts to £1,300,000 a year. The total loss accordingly runs up to £5,200,000 a year.

not be supplied to the artisans in the colony, except in so
far as it could be produced on the tract.

Bellers's ideas secured a better hearing among his successors than among his contemporaries. Robert Owen,
who advanced the same ideas without having been influenced by him, accidentally found an old pamphlet by
Bellers in 1817, and had it printed and a thousand copies
distributed; later on, Karl Marx [69] and in more recent
times Bernstein [70] have referred to the fact that to Bellers
belongs the credit of priority in the formulation of many
of the principles of socialism.

Bellers did not have the good fortune of proving the
correctness of his assertions by a practical test—perhaps,
to be sure, it would be more appropriate to say that he
was spared the disillusionment of seeing them prove false;
for in spite of all his propaganda he did not succeed in
winning over enough people who were able to contribute
capital, and the Quaker workhouse in Clerkenwell was the
only tangible result of his efforts.

Proposals to the Yearly Meetings of 1698 and 1699
led to the formation of a committee of forty-one members
(Bellers was not on the committee, but Thomas Ellwood
is mentioned), and a subscription was taken up which by
1701 had brought in £1923.[71] Later the fund was increased by several legacies. In 1702 the workhouse was
finished, within the limits of the meeting at St. James in

---

[69] Marx, in *Das Kapital* (references are to translation from third
German edition, by Samuel Moore and Edward Aveling, London 1904),
calls Bellers "a very phenomenon in the history of political economy,"
(p. 494, *note*). He refers to him elsewhere: see pp. 107, 115, 122 (*notes*).
[70] See Bernstein, *op. cit.* (see note 53), pp. 276, 282.
[71] Yearly Meeting Minutes, and Trust Property Books.

POOR RELIEF

Clerkenwell,[72] and the Quarterly Meeting of London and Middlesex made report of 178 poor persons and 53 children whose acceptance there was to be considered.

Care at this house was not given free; the monthly meeting, on the contrary, was obligated to pay regularly one shilling a week for children (in addition to which an entrance fee of 40 shillings was charged from 1750 on), and from 1s. 6d. to 3s. 6d. a week for adults—a price which marked a considerable saving in comparison with the cost of public maintenance of the poor. Thus, for instance in the minutes of the Monthly Meeting of Southwark for November 6, 1706, there is the record that thirty persons, unable to support themselves, had been supported in the workhouse at a yearly cost of £130, though these thirty would have received cash contributions for their support in their own homes amounting to £300, "exclusive of the costs of coals and rent."

The cheapness of the maintenance made possible by operating on a greater scale was occasionally taken advantage of by persons who were not entirely destitute, but could themselves make the required payment. Requests of this nature to the monthly meetings can apparently be taken as evidence that a stay in Clerkenwell was considered relatively pleasant, and that the house did not have the character of a place of forcible detention, as did the public workhouses. To be sure, a twelve-hour working day was maintained, so far as the inmates were capable of it, though intermissions amounting to an hour and a half

[72] On the history of the Quaker workhouse, see *An Account of the rise, progress, and present state, of the school and workhouse maintained by the people called Quakers at Clerkenwell*, London 1746, and *Saffron Walden School, a Sketch of Two Hundred Years*, London 1902.

were allowed for meals, and children had two more hours set aside for elementary instruction. The occupation consisted of spinning wool and cotton, winding silk, etc. If the inmates had previously worked at a given trade, this work was continued.

The goods manufactured were probably sold for the most part to members of the Society, who were frequently admonished to support the workhouse with their orders. Occasionally complaints were made that the inmates were not sufficiently industrious; but the introduction of money fines brought about an improvement in this respect. In spite of this, the house did not, in the long run, prove profitable; small surpluses in the early years were followed from 1740 on by fairly large deficits, which were met by the subscription of new funds.

The institution was managed by a committee, the members of which met for regular meetings at the house and also visited there between meetings. Besides this the women had the duty of visiting the poor of their district who were in the workhouse, encouraging them to be industrious, and, in case of need, receiving any complaints about their conduct. This good custom, however, does not seem to have been kept up very long, and the Quarterly Meeting of 1750 proposes anew the naming of such a committee of visitors; in 1805 the name of Elizabeth Fry appears on the list of women appointed.

A few years later, in 1811, the workhouse as such ceased to exist; though not until it had undergone several changes of character. Even as early as 1706 the proposal had been made that the labor of the older inmates should not be reckoned as a source of support for the institution, because of the small value of the work they could do (the return from such work amounted on the average to only half a farthing a day). From that time the stronger inmates were supposed to bear the burden of the care of the weaker ones who needed help, and the institution was therefore to be considered an asylum for the aged and a workhouse for children. This plan was not, however, carried out; nor was the plan (records of which appear in 1712) for establishing a factory; for it did not appear that the strength of the inmates was sufficient to enable them to be set to work at a profit. In the course of the years the working time of the children was more and more cut down in favor of school instruction, and finally ceased altogether,[73] so that the plan of continuing the institution merely as an ordinary school, officially adopted in 1811, really only confirmed a situation which was already in existence, and the only change effected by it was that the section devoted to old people was given up. The last seven inmates of this section were sent back to their home meetings, to be cared for in some other way.[74]

The abandonment of the workhouse as such is not to be regarded as proof that Bellers's plan could not be carried out. Persons within the age limits best adapted to productive labor, whose strength and skill Bellers wished

[73] But not with the purpose of raising the children above the level of the working class. Girls, for instance, were to be trained exclusively as domestic servants. Instruction in skilled handiwork, which was started, was abandoned, because too great skill might awaken undesirable ambitions.

[74] At its opening the institution received more adults than children. Within the first few decades, however, the ratio seems to have changed, and it is to be supposed that, especially in Clerkenwell, a large number of orphans were received, since nothing is known of any institution designed for orphans alone.

primarily to utilize, were never made inmates of the work-house; and besides, the agrarian basis upon which he planned to set up his colony was wholly lacking at Clerkenwell.

Another undertaking was started at about the same time (1696) by the Quaker group in Bristol,[75] and prospered somewhat better than the institution in Clerkenwell, though it cannot be shown that it was due to Bellers's influence. The purpose of this undertaking was "to provide employment for poor Friends at weaving cloth."[76] The excellent fabrics made here were in demand among dealers in all parts of England; but in spite of this the factory was closed down in 1720. The house has been used since then as a home for the indigent poor, and for various other charitable purposes, i.e., as a soup kitchen, a kindergarten, etc.

The fact that these two institutions (namely, at Clerkenwell and at Bristol) maintained their original character only a relatively short time may perhaps be due to the same cause: the need which they were created to fill ceased to be acute. The first half of the eighteenth century was a period of economic expansion—primarily of agricultural expansion—in England; prices of the means of subsistence dropped, while wages rose.[77] During this

[75] Bristol, about the year 1700, was the second greatest industrial and commercial city of England, with about 29,000 inhabitants. It was the seat of a large Quaker community.

[76] Trust Property Books of Bristol and Somerset Quarterly Meeting.

[77] Rogers, *op. cit.* (see note 1), p. 270. Malthus also mentions the general contentment and comfort of the people during the reign of George II (1727-1760), "the happiest period of English history." See *Drei Schriften über die Getreidezölle aus den Jahren 1814 and 1815* (Three essays on the taxes on grain in the years 1814 and 1815), edited by Leeser, Leipzig 1896, Introduction p. xvii.

period, there was a marked decrease in poverty among the Quakers—partly as a result of these generally favorable conditions, and partly because the conscientious carrying out of the above-mentioned policies of the monthly meetings not only improved the status of their own members, but discouraged an influx of members from among the destitute classes. It worked so as to frighten off those who were too lazy to work, but it also kept out many an ambitious worker who did not care to expose himself to the suspicion of wishing to be taken in for the sake of material advantages.[78]

Although it is not possible to determine in detail from what sources the membership was recruited, it is still safe to say that it became increasingly homogeneous as time went on. This does not mean that the Society consisted exclusively of well-to-do persons,[79] but the majority of the members belonged to that part of the middle class that was in fairly comfortable circumstances: farmers [80] and artisans were gradually replaced by merchants, who sometimes worked their way up to the status of capitalists and bankers [81] and from whose number there arose also some distinguished men of science.

But while the economic level of the Society rose, the

[78] Referred to by the Society itself in *An Appeal on the Subject of membership in the Society of Friends.*

[79] The fact that no Quaker ever applied for public charity caused this belief to be widely held. The minutes on poverty, which are to be found in every period of Quaker history, prove its erroneousness.

[80] Rogers, *op. cit.,* p. 85, shows that Quakers have been of notable service to agriculture. The rigorous collection of the church tithes, which Quakers for reasons of conscience refused to pay, gradually drove the Quakers entirely out of the practice of agriculture.

[81] The Quakers made out best as merchants and bankers, since through their absolute reliability they won the confidence of the public. The introduction of the one-price system of selling is credited to them.

quality of their inner life suffered some deterioration."
There was no noticeable neglect of the poor—the requirement of annual reports concerning the system of poor
relief prevented that; but the personal interest in the
needy decreased. An evidence of this is the emphasis upon
the absolutely voluntary character of their care of the
poor, as well as the correspondences between meetings,
which arose in the eighteenth century and were often pro-
longed to weary lengths, regarding the question as to
which meeting was liable for many of the cases requiring
support. The disappearance of the community feeling
indicates a retrogression in respect to religious life. Quakerism had lost its power to attract outsiders to membership, and when a religious body like the Society of Friends
is obliged to depend upon the birth of children within its
membership as the main source of its new members, it
cannot be sure of maintaining a succession of persons well
fitted to bear the burden of leadership.

Still enough of the old spirit remained to regenerate
Quakerism from within. The Yearly Meeting strictly
and persistently opposed every tendency toward a weakening of the religious and social life, which seemed
endangered primarily by the money-getting spirit.[83]
Wealth, it warned, leads to luxury, which is especially
harmful to the younger generation. Simplicity was therefore made a duty incumbent upon the rich, since the rich
man is only a steward of wealth entrusted to him by God.

[82] *Journal* of John Griffith, London 1779: "Friends seemed too much at
ease in a profession; when this is the case, the life of religion is exceed-
ingly depressed."
[83] The following statements rest mainly upon the Yearly Meeting
Epistles.

POOR RELIEF

While special warnings are issued of the dangers of wealth, moderation is held up as worthy of the highest esteem.[84] Increased demands should be met rather by frugality than by extension of one's business activity, since the latter may easily involve the property of others in some sort of risk. All undertakings in which the speculative element plays any part [85] are vigorously condemned. Gain without corresponding labor cannot be reconciled with the observance of the strictest honesty such as is required of the Quakers. Again and again the meeting holds up as examples the first Friends, who always met their obligations to the government (by paying all levies and taxes) and to their fellow citizens (by punctually paying all their debts), and still found more time for labors of love than their successors. The Yearly Meeting sought to secure its ends by these admonitions, and also by sending weighty Friends to visit all the meetings (1760).

It was soon plain, from the renewal of humanitarian activity, that the efforts to reawaken the sort of piety that had been characteristic of the early Quakers were having

[84] Repeatedly referred to in the Epistles, and elsewhere; for instance, see *An Appeal on the Subject of the Accumulation of Wealth Addressed to the Society of Friends* . . ., 2d edition London 1824.

[85] The fever of speculation which seized multitudes of people in England at this time makes the disapproval of the Quakers easily intelligible. From the twenties of the eighteenth century on, numerous fraudulent enterprises (the so-called bubbles) arose; there were even cases in which the purpose of the proposed company was not announced at the time of its organization, and shares were sold in "an undertaking which shall be in due time revealed." The low price of the shares of stock (as low as 2s. 6d.) occasioned their sale among all classes of society. The immense demand for such shares often drove the market price up to ten or twenty times the par value. See Macpherson, *op. cit.* (see above, note 13), iii, 90ff.

their effect. They did not limit themselves thereafter to the circle of their own meetings, where all they could do was to maintain the status quo, but turned their attention more and more to those outside their membership who were in need. At the same time individual members of the Society were active as doers of deeds of charity, independently of the organization as such.

From the abundance of the labors that were performed, isolated instances can be cited. In its official capacity the Society worked primarily through the formation of committees for the mitigation of extreme cases of destitution. Their care was sometimes called forth by the crying need of helping prisoners of war or noncombatants who had suffered through war; [86] sometimes by the oppressed or often absolutely desperate condition of the English laboring class.

The meetings turned their attention for the most part to great groups of the needy, and were obliged to satisfy themselves with rendering occasional assistance; but the individual Quaker had an opportunity, within a limited field of activity, to apply the more fundamental principles of his Society's theory of poor relief—the prevention of pauperism and assistance toward self-help. Through the experience which the Quakers had gained in living as members of a community, they seemed especially well fitted to contribute to the solution of many of the problems which were brought before the political economist by

[86] Thus, to mention two cases, in 1806 the Quakers took up a subscription for the benefit of Germans, "to rescue our fellow-men who are literally ready to perish," and in 1870 a War Victims' Fund was formed "for the relief of the Peasantry and other non-combattant sufferers in France and Germany."

the rapid economic decline during the last of the eighteenth century.

The distress of the lower classes in England at this time was almost as great as in the middle of the seventeenth century. War, crop failures, and fundamental changes in economic life, brought about by such factors as the introduction of machinery, the growth of large-scale industries, and renewed inclosures [87] of public lands on an extensive scale, caused a great increase in the number of the needy, and hence in the amount of the contributions required for their support.[88] Mitigation of the severity of the poor laws, even though it was welcome as an indication of an increasingly humane attitude,[89] had the general effect of bringing the whole working class down to the level of the lowest paid laborer. In 1782, Gilbert's Act [90] had repealed the so-called workhouse test (that is, it was forbidden thereafter by law to send any person to the workhouse [91] who was not ill or incapacitated); the

[87] The second period of inclosing common land, from 1760 to 1830, was for the purpose of more intensive cultivation of the soil. See Toynbee, *op. cit.* (see above, note 6), p. 88ff.

[88] A quotation from the reports of various parishes, which were compiled at the instance of the House of Commons, shows that the number of persons supported at public expense increased from an estimated 294,786 in 1785 to an estimated 2,079,432 in 1812 (*The Philanthropist*, ii, 312 and iii, 46-47). The records differ as to the accompanying rise in the poor rate: in 1785 it was 5s. per capita of population, with an expenditure on account of the poor of £1,943,649; in 1813 it was 12s. 8d. per capita of population, which would be the equivalent of an annual yield of about £7,000,000. See Nicholls, *op. cit.*, ii, 302. By way of comparison observe that in 1896, after an enormous increase in population, the yield from the poor rate was only £7,500,000.

[89] See Anton von Kostanecki, *Arbeit und Armut* (Work and poverty), Freiburg (in Breisgau) 1909, p. 149; Nicholls, *op. cit.*, ii, 64.

[90] 22 George III. c. 83; see Nicholls, *op. cit.*, ii, 89.

[91] Hereafter the workhouses were accordingly to be designated as "poorhouses"; see Nicholls, *op. cit.*, ii, 92.

poor who could work acquired the right to claim employment in the vicinity of their places of residence. This
soon led to the policy of eking out insufficient incomes by
means of a system of doles or allowances, by which a
depressing effect was brought to bear upon the whole level
of wages, and more and more laborers sank into a condition of economic dependence.[92]

Among the numerous proposals for the permanent
amelioration of this discreditable condition, the essay of
the Quaker William Allen (1780-1840) is of especial
interest to us: *Colonies at Home: or, the Means for rendering the industrious labourer independent of Parish
relief*, Lindfield 1832. Like other authors before and
after him,[93] he considers that the chief cause of all ills is
the withdrawal of population from the land to the cities,
and tries to bring about the establishment of home colonies by a scheme of giving out lots for cultivation under
expert direction. "The most natural and healthiest occupation for man is the cultivation of the soil; and both rich
and poor are in the end dependent upon it for the maintenance of their lives." There are exhaustive proposals

[92] The so-called allowance system was introduced by law in 1796 by
36 George III. c. 10 and 23, though in fact it had existed earlier. Not
until 1832 was the allowance in addition to the wage abolished, by 2 and
3 William IV. c. 96; see Nicholls, *op. cit.*, ii, 123, 227.

[93] Even Defoe had lamented the broad unused expanses of land (D.
Defoe and S. Richardson, *A Tour through the Island of Great Britain,*
8th edition London 1778, iii, 176), while the ordinary necessities were
dear. The *Reports* of the Society for Bettering the Condition of the Poor
draw attention repeatedly to the significance of ownership by the laborer
of his plot of ground as a means of improving his condition. The value
of personally owned plots in supplying productive employment to laborers
out of work is also stressed by W. H. Saunders (*An Address . . . upon
the Practical Means of gradually Abolishing the Poor Laws . . .*, London
1821).

with regard to the types of person best suited for the
colony—not only unskilled laborers but also artisans and
farmers are considered desirable—and with regard to
various plans of administration according to the amount
of capital invested. Allen, thanks to his scientific knowledge (he was a chemist of some note), can give valuable
suggestions regarding fertilizing the land, rotation of
crops, feeding the livestock, and (not the least important)
the economical and wholesome nourishment of human
beings. He expects especially good results for Ireland
from the establishment of such colonies: according to his
view, the means of subsistence could be so much increased
by them that emigration would be unnecessary. The cost
of emigration, hitherto estimated at £60 for each family,
would pay for settlement in a colony.

The published propaganda was followed by the practical demonstration. A training farm [94] was started first in
Lindfield, Sussex, with which workshops of various kinds
were associated. Shortly afterwards, through the liberality of a local sympathizer, it had become possible
to erect twenty-five laborers' cottages, with a suitable
plot of farming land for each one; and the result
was completely satisfactory even at a time in which
there was very little practical knowledge of scientific
farming.[95]

In spite of the fact that the experiment met with almost
startling success, and the royal family, who visited the

[94] Often called an "industrial school." Allen supported this school
liberally until his death. See *Life of William Allen, with Selections from
his Correspondence*, Philadelphia 1847, ii, 149, 161, 206.
[95] See James Sherman, *Memoir of William Allen*, Philadelphia [1851],
p. 398ff.

colony in 1831, expressed the greatest satisfaction with it,[96] the extension which had been hoped for to wider fields did not take place. For a time Allen worked for such extension in England and on the Continent; but numerous other duties made it impossible to promote this project very energetically. Allen is thus a good example of the Quaker philanthropist: along with the exacting duties of his profession he attended indefatigably to the cure or elimination of social ills. When we come to consider education, prison reform, and the antislavery agitation, we shall refer to his services again. As organ of the various proposals for the advancement of human welfare he published a magazine, *The Philanthropist*, from 1811 on.

At the same time Allen lent his aid to the most varied efforts aiming at the relief of emergency cases of want. Quakers who were in industry on a large scale were among those who were authorized organizers of such joint efforts. Thus in 1810, during a severe crisis of the English silk industry (a consequence of stoppage of the supply of raw silk) the silk dealer Peter Bedford [97] established the Spitalfields Soup Society and the Spitalfields Association for the Relief of Special Cases of Distress among the Industrious Poor. He secured the coöperation of a great number of men and women for this labor of love; and each worker was assigned a territory in Spitalfields, the central point of the London silk industry. Within their assigned territories, the members of these

[96] Even the *Times* spoke very appreciatively of Allen's plans, and approved of his condemnation of the allowance system.

[97] See William Tallack, *Peter Bedford, the Spitalfields Philanthropist*, London 1865.

associations did what they could to save the starving population from dying of hunger, by gifts of food, by better administration of the buying and selling of foodstuffs, and by finding work for the unemployed.

The formation of such an association was at that time something absolutely new for most people; but for the Quakers it was only an imitation of the plan which they used for caring for the poor within their own meetings. The move to extend the plan further was made by Elizabeth Fry.[98] She established a District Visiting Society in Brighton in 1834, exactly according to Quaker principles, the purpose of whose members was to promote industry and thrift among the poor by visiting them in their homes, and to extend help where they found any cases of real want, but at the same time to exercise care that the liberality of those who were willing to give was not abused. Her example was followed in many places, as her labors were attended by good success. This same woman labored to make the status of the servant more secure by founding a National Guardian Association (1825), the purpose of which was to act as employment bureau, to give help in case of need, and to care for the aged. This last aim was to be attained as far as possible through education in thrift, not through the giving out of doles from the funds of the Association.

Mention should also be made of the part which the

[98] On Elizabeth Fry see the following: *Memoir of the Life of Elizabeth Fry* . . . edited by two of her daughters, 2 vols., Philadelphia 1847; Georgina King Lewis, *Elizabeth Fry,* London 1906 (German edition by F. Siegmund Schulze, Stiftungsverlag, Potsdam 1911); William H. Render, *Through Prison Bars: the Lives and Labours of John Howard and Elizabeth Fry* . . ., London [1894]. See the account of Elizabeth Fry's labors in behalf of prison reform in Chapter V of the present work.

Quakers took in the maintenance of the colony in New
Lanark. Its founder, David Dale, was not a Quaker, to
be sure, but allied to the Quakers in his way of thinking
and acting. Through his numerous charitable activities
he had brought it about that not a single one of a group
of more than 2,000 spinners applied for public charity
during the many years of this period of economic depression, nor was any guilty of a crime. After Dale's death,
Robert Owen attempted to carry on the enterprise, but
was not able to do so from his own resources; and William Allen, Joseph Fox and John Walker lent their aid by
becoming joint owners.[99] Owen retained the management of the business, while the others, who were Quakers,
concentrated their attention upon the care of the workers,
especially the children.[100]

Moreover, all the plans which aimed at lowering the
cost of living helped toward the creation of maintenance of wholesome conditions among the working class.
Bedford's organization, mentioned above, for providing
the lower classes with food, had been preceded, and was
followed, by others of the same kind. John Fothergill
(1712-1780) [101] was already busying himself with devel-
oping high-grade fish and potatoes, and was spreading the
idea of partially substituting maize for the expensive
wheat; but the movement which finally did away with
monopoly prices, that for *free trade,* had its roots in

[99] See Sherman, *op. cit.,* pp. 102ff., 136, 137, 181ff., 395.

[100] Owen's liberal views later brought him into serious conflict with
the Quakers, in which the latter had their way: instruction in the Christian religion was retained. On the colony at Lanark see Robert Owen,
A New View of Society, London 1813-14.

[101] See James H. Tuke, *A Sketch of the Life of John Fothergill,* published by the Centenary Committee, Ackworth School 1879.

Quakerism, and received great assistance from Quakers. Not only was John Bright a Quaker (one of the first to enter Parliament); there were many Quakers on the membership list of the Anti-Corn-Law League (as, for example, Joseph Sturge,[102] who supplied moral and religious backing to the movement); and this organization is said to have been influential in causing the adoption of the policy of not being content with compromise measures.[103]

Many individual Quaker employers doubtless put into effect plans for the welfare of their employees without joining any recognized organization for this purpose; but it is hard to determine how much they accomplished. The excellent understanding and good feeling between Quakers and their employees is praised on many sides. Thus William Forster,[104] a Quaker woolen manufacturer in Bradford, who also felt a lively sympathy with the Chartist movement, is reckoned as the only owner of a spinning establishment who was ever regarded by the workmen as their friend. Carlyle, too, in his writings on political economy, sets up a Quaker as the ideal type of employer, and recommends that his methods be used as widely as possible.[105]

[102] See *Memoirs of Joseph Sturge,* by Henry Richard, London 1864.
[103] It cannot be said with certainty whether or not the Rochdale pioneers (in consumers' coöperation) were Quakers, or had any connection with Quakerism. It seems possible that this first attempt to organize a plan whereby the individual consumers should themselves manage the business of merchandizing their necessities was started in imitation of similar organizations set up by philanthropists for their benefit.
[104] See T. Wemyss Reid, *Life of the Right Honourable William Edward Forster,* London 1888.
[105] Thomas Carlyle, *Past and Present,* bk. iv, ch. 5, in *Works,* Literary edition, 30 vols., London 1869-71, xiii, 343.

THE QUAKERS AS PIONEERS

In these days, in view of the generally increased interest in the lower classes, it is hardly possible for the Quakers to maintain their lead as pioneers in any branch of poor relief. But there are hardly any organized efforts made toward social betterment in which they have not taken part. For instance, as an example from most recent times, we may refer to the solution of the housing problem for a multitude of industrial workers through the establishment of the garden city of Bournville by George Cadbury.[106]

Whatever was undertaken, expression was given to the desire to create *humane and dignified conditions of living,* even for the man who had no property, *as the first prerequisite of morality and religious life.*

[106] According to the report of the Bournville Village Trust for 1907, the garden city comprised 669 houses with 3,170 inhabitants. These are by no means exclusively employees of the firm of Cadbury: about 60% of them have positions in other places, mostly in Birmingham. The public health in the colony is extraordinarily good: the death rate is only 50% of the average death rate for England.

CHAPTER TWO

EDUCATION

THE necessity of improving and extending education among the masses was first agitated in England by the Puritans; for since they declined to admit the theory that the clergy should stand in the relation of spiritual guardians to the laity, and do all their thinking for them, they were obliged to reckon with the necessity of bringing up each individual person so that he should have the power of independent judgment. This is the general tendency of Milton's proposal to apply the ecclesiastical estates which had been seized by the crown to the establishment of a great number of schools and public libraries throughout the country.[1] Harrington [2] goes even further: in *Oceana* he adopts the modern idea of free compulsory schooling under state control [3]—a plan which, as is well known, did not reach full fruition in England till 1870.

This notion, which was held by the Puritans generally, acquires special significance among the Quakers. They carry through to its logical conclusion the theory of independence in matters of faith; and hence they believe

[1] See Alfred Stern, *Milton und seine Zeit* (Milton and his time), Leipzig 1877, II, iii, 216, 217.
[2] James Harrington (1611-1677), an English political philosopher whose principal work, *Oceana* (1656), describes an ideal state.
[3] See Charles Firth, *Oliver Cromwell and the Rule of the Puritans in England,* London 1900, p. 354.

that religious conviction rests jointly on feeling and reason. Further, the close connection between intellectual growth and economic security afforded an incentive for the careful education of the next generation.

In carrying out this plan the first Friends were dependent entirely upon their own resources. They would not consider instruction in the public schools any more than they would consider public poor relief; and besides, they would not have sent their children to either public or private schools, for reasons of religion. And so they had the task of providing schools in which instruction was possible on a foundation of Quaker faith, and of making them accessible to all by granting loans of money or, in case of need, by assuming the whole cost themselves.

It very soon came about that different principles were followed in their educational system from those which we found in our discussion of their care of the poor. Whereas in the matter of poor relief publicity was resorted to with the intent of discouraging unworthy applicants, and the emphasis was continually laid upon the duty of self-support, in the matter of education of children there was never any suggestion that those of limited means should be satisfied with less than the best.[4]

In regard to education, the Society owed much to the ideas of Fox, Penn and Bellers. All three hoped to see the formation of a unified educational system; but they differed in the requirements that they laid down for such a system. However, as the decisions of the Yearly Meet-

[4] The duty of parents to lay before the meeting their needs for their children's education is often referred to, and the meeting was made jointly responsible with the parents. Annual reports on education were rendered to the Yearly Meeting.

ing were subject to influence now from one side and now from another, and the practice differed even from the theory as laid down, it is impossible to speak of a Quaker school system as such (at least not until the middle of the nineteenth century), or to describe it in general terms, as has occasionally been attempted.

The earliest pronouncement by Fox of which we have a record, regarding the education of children, is contained in a pamphlet of the year 1657.[5] In this the principal emphasis is laid upon religious instruction; all the "worldly arts," such as music, dancing, and the like, should be avoided. Fox, however, by no means recommended a one-sided development, adapted only to a future state, to the exclusion of proper attention to the practical requirements of this present world. This is evidenced by the establishment of two schools in 1667, one in Waltham for boys, one in Shacklewell for girls, in which the children were to learn "whatsoever things were civil and useful in the creation." [6]

Unfortunately we have no more detailed explanation of how this was to be attained. Even in his reports of certain other schools, the private enterprises of individual Quakers, Fox makes no mention of the subjects taught. On the other hand, we know that in 1674 the Six Weeks' Meeting was instructed to establish a school for the free education of the children of poor members; "the master was to be one well skilled in Latin, writing, and arithmetic." [7]

[5] *A Warning to all Teachers of Children which are called School-Masters and School-Mistresses, and to Parents . . .*, London 1657.
[6] *Journal,* ii, 89. See also Beck and Ball, p. 360.
[7] Beck and Ball, p. 131.

THE QUAKERS AS PIONEERS

Thus the Quakers offered instruction in Latin to the poorest children at a time in which the middle class in general throughout the land was still actually illiterate. A little knowledge of Latin was of a certain practical usefulness, to be sure, to the early Quakers, for Latin was the language of the courts of law, and they came into contact very often with the administration of justice. In order for the proper understanding of the administration of justice a textbook seemed desirable from which the children could learn the legal Latin, and in 1675 two Friends were entrusted with the preparation of such a book. In the same year a book for elementary instruction in Latin was published, in the writing of which George Fox [8] had collaborated, and which is interesting to us because of a certain passage in the preface.

The passage in question reads as follows: "We do not exclude anything from the instruction of children, which it is right and useful for them to know—regardless of whether it has reference to Divine matters or is useful for the outward life." The pronouncement may well be taken as a refutation of the reproach often leveled at Quakers, that they belittle education from the fear that knowledge will endanger religious life.

It is true that they denied the necessity of higher education for their ministers, and did not wish their children to become acquainted with heathen authors; the latter wish was even one of the chief reasons for forbidding attendance at the educational institutions of the world.

[8] See Samuel Tuke, *Five Papers on the past Proceedings and Experience of the Society of Friends, in Connection with the Education of Youth,* York 1843, reprinted in *Sketch of the History of Education in the Society of Friends,* York 1855.

EDUCATION

Thus we find in the Epistle of 1690, as also in various
later Epistles: "It is our Christian and earnest advice and
counsel . . . not to send them [your children] to such
schools where they are taught the corrupt ways, manners,
fashions, and language of the world, and of the heathen
in their authors, and the names of the heathenish gods
and goddesses; tending greatly to corrupt and alienate
the minds of children into an averseness or opposition
against the truth, and the simplicity of it." At the same
time the admonition is sent out to "provide schoolmasters
and schoolmistresses who are faithful Friends."

The minutes of the next year [9] show the first summary
of the educational institutions that were then in operation.
Only fifteen schools are mentioned—eleven for boys, two
for girls, two for both boys and girls. Even if allowance
be made for the possible incompleteness of the list (for
from the same minutes it appears that the Yearly Meeting contained 151 monthly meetings), this appears to be
a very small number; though, on the other hand, we must
remember that schools were always boarding schools, and
that many of the congregations were quite small, and
lacked the means to establish such schools.

In the early decades the lack of regular schools was
partly made up for by the practice, followed by many of
the meetings, of arranging for instruction by qualified
members within the meeting house,[10] or of renting rooms
to teachers who set up what amounted to private schools.
The teachers were obliged to arrange with the elders with

[9] Yearly Meeting Minutes for 1691.
[10] Well-known ministers such as William Edmundson, George Whitehead, and George Keith took part in such instructing. *First Publishers
of Truth*, p. 252.

regard to the rate of tuition; the women's meeting often paid for poor children. Beck and Ball's *London Friends' Meetings* (pp. 131, 132) shows that this was customary in the capital, and lists the names of men who opened such schools in the eighties and nineties of the seventeenth century.

The Yearly Meeting is continuously exercised to effect the improvement and extension of juvenile education. Thus in 1695 the hope is expressed [11] that teachers of both sexes may be encouraged in their work, and may come into closer association for mutual consultation about the best pedagogical methods—though this concern had no visible effect, apparently, until 1711, when teachers' conferences began to be held. These conferences, however, were called at the suggestion of the teachers themselves, and were dependent upon plans formed anew each year, for in the interim the interest of the Quakers along educational lines turned more toward the direction of industrial training.

Even as early as 1695 a communication from the Meeting for Sufferings had urgently recommended the establishment of schools in which children "can learn languages and other sciences, and also some remunerative trade, or at least skill and industry, which will contribute to their support and combat many of the temptations associated with idleness." In view of the uncertainty of the status of many of the members of the Society—their conscientious opposition to various of the laws of the land often led to confiscation of their property on a more or less extensive scale—it seemed desirable to observe certain

[11] *Yearly Meeting Epistles,* i, 83.

general principles in teaching which would make the instruction such as would assure a living to rich as well as poor children. Little had been attained in this respect with the general instructions that had been issued so far; the Yearly Meeting therefore named a special committee to consider this weighty problem, and in 1697 received its recommendations.

In these recommendations there is very plain evidence of the influence of Bellers's plans for the establishment of workers' colonies, which had been published the year before. At the same time Bellers addresses an epistle on the education of children directly to his fellow members,[12] which received very large circulation through the efforts of Penn, Ellwood, and other well-known members of the Society. This essay also leads up to the idea of a college of industry. We saw in the preceding chapter to what extent this idea was realized. The combination of manual occupation with instruction is now considered suitable for schools of all sorts: "Children can lessen the cost of their education through their own efforts, and thus (according to Bellers's view) increase their happiness."[13] In case a person without means turns out to have some special gift, he should be able to devote himself exclusively to study, at the expense of the meeting to which he belongs.[14] In 1697 a Friend offers to bear the expense of educating such children to be teachers, if their main-

---

[12] John Bellers, *Epistle to Friends concerning the Education of Children,* 1697.

[13] Bellers is touched, and unpleasantly so, by the truth of the boast of the Dutch that their children manufacture the toys with which the English children play, and in another passage points out that in Germany even the princes learn a trade.

[14] *Sundry Ancient Epistles,* p. 154ff.

tenance during the period of learning is taken care of in some other way.[15]

Aside from such special cases, the predominant idea comes to be that of educating the poorer children to the end that they may later train as apprentices; that is, the attitude toward education, though only within a small area and for a short time, assumes an essentially industrial slant, such as we saw exemplified in the Quaker workhouse at Clerkenwell. It happened in every case, to be sure, that, when indigents were to be trained, the backing of dependable persons was secured, who later interested themselves actively in finding positions for these and other children. In this connection the approval of one of the higher meetings was always necessary; and due attention was paid to the desires and the home situation of the children themselves.[16] In case the family was too poor, the meeting paid the apprenticeship fee,[17] took care of other necessary equipment, and at the close of the training period supplied the apprentice with financial help for setting himself up in business. Funds for this purpose were collected early in Quaker history.[18] The Devonshire House Trust Property Books contain the stipulation that these funds are to be administered apart from the other funds devoted to helping the needy, in order that appro-

[15] Beck and Ball, p. 360, *note*.

[16] See also Fox's letter of 1669, *Journal*, ii, 119.

[17] The amount of this fee is given variously as from £5 to £20. For parish apprentices the average fee in 1747 was £5; in 1793, £10; in 1816, £25.

[18] The General Meeting in London decided as early as 1671, that interest on bequests should be applied to the purpose of "bringing up and putting forth to apprentices Friends' children that are poor, and towards the helping them to set up when their times are out."

priations made from them may not have the character of
alms.

So far as possible, the teachers were supposed to be
members of the Society;[19] in case this could not be arranged, the Society watched over the children with special
care.   In contrast to other members, apprentices gained
residence, and a claim upon the meeting for support, after
forty days within the jurisdiction of the given meeting or
congregation.   Each meeting had the duty of making
reports to the central organization (in this case the Meeting of Twelve) about the apprentices that were placed
out at its expense, including accurate lists of their
names.[20]   Even the contracts of apprenticeship were
drawn up with the help of members of the meeting, and
disputes were settled as far as possible by the meeting,
without appealing to the bureau established by the government for this purpose.

By giving the young people instruction before securing
positions for them as apprentices, by the support and
backing which the meetings afforded, by paying wages
during the period of apprenticeship, and by constant oversight, the Quakers attempted to guard the younger generation from the abuses to which other children in the
same circumstances were exposed.   It was customary, for
instance, for foundlings, especially girls, to be put out as
apprentices at seven years of age, and they often could
not become independent again until their twenty-fifth year.
During this long period they were obliged to use their

[19] Yearly Meeting Minutes for 1697.
[20] Instructions to forward this information were sent out by the Quarterly Meeting at Devonshire House on October 5, 1691.

productive power for the benefit of their masters, without pay for themselves, and often had to put up with harsh or cruel treatment besides.

Similar to the efforts of the English Friends are the methods of education adopted by the earlier Friends in Scotland, Ireland, and Pennsylvania. The minutes of the Quarterly Meeting in Edinburgh held in the Twelfth Month, 1678 (according to present reckoning, February, 1679) contain a record of the intention of the Friends in Aberdeen to establish a public school. This plan was carried out. Two schools were started, and we hear of legacies bequeathed to them and find reports about teachers. In 1711 another school is mentioned, in Ury, the home of the apologist Robert Barclay.[21] In Ireland three so-called "Provincial Schools of Friends" [22] were started at the end of the eighteenth century. It does not appear that much manual labor was required there, although one of the schools is specifically called a school of agriculture (the Brookfield Agricultural School). The sad state of Ireland repeatedly occupied the attention of the Quakers, and they did what they could to improve the condition of the population by educational means.

In Pennsylvania, a consideration of the school situation does not give a proper conception of the ideas entertained by the illustrious Founder about education; but from other sources it has been ascertained that Penn's views

[21] See *Journal of Friends' Historical Society*, September 1910, p. 113.

[22] One school was started in Leinster in 1784, one in Ulster in 1793, and one in Munster in 1794. See *Report concerning Friends' Schools in Ireland*, York 1844, pp. 13, 16, 17: reprinted as an addendum to *Sketch of the History of Education in the Society of Friends*, York 1855.

coincided essentially with those of George Fox. We see from a letter of Penn to his wife [23] that he wished his own children to have the best possible education; and if he appeared to be satisfied with Bellers's ideas for his settlers in Pennsylvania, the reason for this lay in causes which it was not in his power to alter. It is true that a number of academically trained persons went with Penn to the new colony, but the majority of the settlers were very plain people, among whom no sustained urge for higher education made itself felt.[24]

Even though it is true that, for the time being, Pennsylvania remained behind the mother country in respect to its facilities for advanced education, in the extent of its system of elementary education it was far in the lead.[25] The very first laws laid upon all parents the obligation of having their children instructed in reading and writing. On pain of punishment of five pounds, parents were enjoined to see that their children, at the end of the twelfth year, were able to read the Bible, and to write.[26] After that, instruction in a trade or some other useful business was to be begun, "to the end none may be idle, but the poor may work to live, and the rich, if they become poor,

[23] See Elizabeth Braithwaite Emmott, *The Story of Quakerism,* London 1908, p. 150. Penn instructs his wife to spare no expense in the education of their children; along with academic training the learning of a trade was thought desirable.

[24] The Puritans had founded Harvard as early as 1636. The University of Pennsylvania, on the contrary, was not established until 1746-55, and was not essentially due to the efforts of Quakers. It owed much, for instance, to Benjamin Franklin.

[25] Isaac Sharpless, *A Quaker Experiment in Government,* Philadelphia 1898, i, 35ff; Thomas Woody, *Early Quaker Education in Pennsylvania,* New York 1920.

[26] Sharpless, *op. cit.,* p. 37.

may not want."[27] Consideration for the education of children was the chief reason, in the opinion of Daniel Pastorius, founder of Germantown, for Penn's insistence that new settlements should be made only in units of township size.[28]

The governor and legislature [29] appointed teachers and determined the tuition fees. In 1683, scarcely a year after the establishment of the city, steps were taken to open a school,[30] and as early as 1689 a public Latin school was established on the model of an English grammar school, which still exists under the name William Penn Charter School. Private individuals followed with the establishment of other schools for higher education. It is noteworthy that the schools were everywhere predominantly coeducational.[31] It may be safely assumed that instruction in the elementary grades was actually given to all children, rich and poor alike; for the community expected, as a matter of course, to contribute assist-

[27] Penn's *Frame of Government* (1682), Article xxviii, reprinted in *Minutes of the Provincial Council of Pennsylvania*, Philadelphia 1852, i, 40.

[28] See Marion Dexter Learned, *The Life of Francis Daniel Pastorius*, Philadelphia 1908, p. 172.

[29] Committee of Manners, Education and Arts.

[30] *The Minutes of the Provincial Council* for Oct. 26, 1683 (i, 91) record the concern of the Governor and council to provide for the "instruction and sober education of youth," and their engagement of Enoch Flower as teacher, and their agreement with him as to the fees to be charged for tuition and for board. The *Minutes* for Nov. 17, 1683 (i, 93) contain the following notice: "Proposed that care be Taken about the Learning and Instruction of Youth, to Witt: A Scool of Arts and Siences."

[31] Whether coeducation was introduced as a matter of necessity, resulting from the lack of funds sufficient for the maintenance of separate schools for boys and girls, or was adopted as a matter of principle, has not been determined. The English Quakers did not declare themselves in favor of the principle of coeducation until the nineteenth century.

ance to any school in need of it, just as in the old country, and to help in the education of the poorer children.

The efforts of the Quakers along educational lines were not directed only toward the white settlers. About 1770 schools for colored people were started—for slaves as well as free persons, for both sexes and all ages—in which both instruction and school supplies were free. Except for the voluntary contributions of a few slave owners, these schools were maintained by subscriptions and gifts from Quakers.[22]

We will now return to England and consider the further development of the educational system of the Quakers during the eighteenth century. The Yearly Meeting made vigorous efforts to see that all children attended school—down to 1740 the admonition to set up and maintain schools is repeatedly sent out; but the individual monthly meetings fell far short of this goal. The school system at the beginning of the eighteenth century had made striking progress, it is true, as regards the number of schools; for even as early as 1709 the reports to the Yearly Meeting indicate that there were very few monthly meetings in which there was not either a meeting school or some other specific provision for the education of the young. Nevertheless, it appears probable that in most of the meetings the demand for education exceeded the supply.

The urgent admonition of the Epistle of 1701 that no child should be obliged to go without a school education because of poverty, occasioned difficulty, because the schools then in existence, with the exception of those in

[22] Taken from English reports on Pennsylvania.

the workhouses at Clerkenwell and Bristol, were too expensive. The employment of children in gainful occupations had probably proved to be unsatisfactory. Indeed,
it probably had never actually been tried on any large
scale; at any rate, Bellers reported in 1718 that children
could not be accepted in the training schools in London
for less than £18 or £20, and in the North not under £8
or £10; whereas most parents were unable to put up more
than £5. Various attempts were made to help out the
needy, but the means were insufficient. For instance, subscriptions were invited for a fund from which teachers
were to receive a bonus for every pupil, as an incentive to
the establishment of private schools. The zeal for undertakings on a large scale had diminished; even when so
important a matter as the training of the young was involved, there was a perceptible sentiment in the second
generation of Quakers that the observation of the church
discipline in trifling matters, if strictly enforced, would
absorb a disproportionate amount of time and effort.

It is not likely that children of well-to-do parents were
obliged to go without schooling at this time, although it
occasionally happened that a communication from the
Yearly Meeting was sent out urging more thorough education. Thus in 1737 the learning of a foreign language,
as French, Dutch, or Danish, was recommended, with a
view to its use in business;[33] and in 1759 an attempt was
made to meet the objections which some Friends raised
to too much learning, as follows: "Even the best things
are capable of being abused; but that is no fault of the
things themselves. It cannot be shown that human knowl-

[33] Yearly Meeting Minutes for 1737.

EDUCATION

edge is a hindrance to religious progress; Isaac Penington, Robert Barclay, and William Penn had a many-sided
spiritual training."[34]

After exhaustive study of the existing need of schools,[35]
and as a result of many admonitions on the part of the
Yearly Meeting, the Quarterly Meeting in Yorkshire
finally led the way, toward the end of the seventies, with
the establishment of a large educational institution for
"children of parents not in affluence." This was Ackworth School, which still exists, and which owes its foundation in no little measure to the efforts of the philanthropic
physician John Fothergill (1712-1780).[36] He negoti-
ated the advantageous purchase of a building in 1778,[37]
and a year later the new school stood ready for 314 children. The expense of instruction and care amounted in
the beginning to £8.8s. annually. At this price private
benefactors could secure a "bill of admission" for a
child.[38] Whatever amount in excess of this sum was spent
on each child (for the price charged was never sufficient
to meet the expenses) had to be raised by subscription.[39]

In the interests of economy, and to secure the small
resulting income, the policy was revived of putting the
children to work, especially as Fothergill advised that

[34] Meeting for Sufferings, 1759.
[35] Undertaken by the Meeting for Sufferings, 1759-60.
[36] See James H. Tuke, *A Sketch of the Life of John Fothergill . . .*,
1879; R. Hingston Fox, *Dr. John Fothergill and his Friends,* London 1919.
[37] It had been erected in the reign of George III as a foundling
asylum, but had been in use only a short time. The cost of building was
reputed to have been £17,000, but the purchase price paid by the
Quakers amounted to only £7,000.
[38] By 1848 the prices charged ranged from £18 to £48, according to
the circumstances of the parents.
[39] The Quarterly Meeting of London and Middlesex contributed more
than twice as much as any other quarterly meeting.

physical labor should be combined with school instruction for the sake of the children's health. The boys were given thorough instruction in the three R's, and in addition had to do garden work and a few domestic chores. For the girls, on the other hand, in the beginning, the only instruction was in needlework and housekeeping, "as is suitable to their sex and position"; though this differentiation is obviously in conflict with the theory, usually maintained by the Quakers, of the equality of the sexes. We can form an idea of the demands made on their industry from the fact that they sewed all the linen and some of the other clothing for the whole body of pupils, and besides this knitted all their stockings and even prepared work of better grade for sale.

Only gradually did more emphasis come to be placed upon formal book instruction. Improvement in the religious instruction came about in the first instance from the impetus given by Joseph John Gurney, to whom the school owes a great deal in other ways; then came an improvement in the quality of scientific instruction by division into classes; and finally the need for recreation was recognized and sports introduced into the school.

Even under these conditions the life the children led was not exactly enviable. Their clothing and the care they received were extraordinarily simple, the heating of the house entirely insufficient. The children were shut off from the world as if they lived in a convent; until 1847 there were not even any vacations. The cost of traveling to and from the school, which for most children would have been considerable, was a principal reason for keep-

EDUCATION

ing them there continuously. The pupils thus usually
remained away from their parents from four to seven
years; and many did not return to their families even
after finishing their schooling, as they were obliged to
take a position at once. According to Rowntree, leaving
home in order to enter school often meant a parting for
life.[40] Even correspondence by letter between parents
and children was almost impossible, on account of the
high postage rates.

This strict training corresponded to Penn's principles,
as he expressed them in his *Reflections and Maxims* (part
2, §142ff.) : [41] "Children can't be too hardly bred: For
beside that it fits them to bear the Roughest Providences,
it is more Masculine, Active, and Healthy. Nay, 'tis certain, that the Liberty of the Mind is mightily preserved
by it. . . . The memory of the Ancients is hardly in any
Thing more to be celebrated, than in a Strict and Useful
Institution of Youth. By Labour they prevented Luxury
in their young People, till wisdom and Philosophy had
taught them to resist and despise it."

The pedagogical results in Ackworth were altogether
good; [42] it is thought that the very great falling off in poverty among the Quakers in the nineteenth century is in

[40] Phebe Doncaster, *John Stephenson Rowntree, His Life and Work*,
London 1908, containing (p. 301ff.) J. S. Rowntree's *A Sketch of the History of Ackworth School, 1779-1879*. On Ackworth School see also Henry
Thompson, *A History of Ackworth School during its first Hundred years*,
London 1879; and Thomas Pumphrey, *History of Ackworth School*, Ackworth 1853.
[41] William Penn, *Some Fruits of Solitude in Reflections and Maxims*,
1st edition London 1693; citation from edition by John Clifford, London
1905, p. 138.
[42] Reports on the School by Dr. Fothergill, 1780, and Sarah Grubb, 1786.

large measure due to this School.[43] To be sure, opposing
this view, the objection is sometimes made, even by
Quakers, that the School occupied itself too much with
training a population of laborers, and did not devote
enough attention to the possibility of supplying the later
need for professional people of various kinds; but it is a
fact, as can be shown, that several distinguished men
passed their childhood in Ackworth. Among these, to
name only a few, we may mention the parliamentarian
John Bright, and James Wilson, founder of the *Economist* and minister of finance in India.

In the nineteenth century there arose a number of other
schools under the care of meetings, which met the
requirements of more advanced education.[44] The educational department of the workhouse in Clerkenwell,
which, as was pointed out above, was maintained only as
a school from 1811 on, developed in the course of time
into one of the best institutions in England for the middle
and upper classes, and, after various changes of location,
exists to-day in Saffron Walden, bearing the name of the
town in which it is located. In 1836 the Quakers founded
an association devoted specifically to educational matters

---

[43] There were private foundations of similar type. For instance, in
1785 Leonard Raw, of Reeth, Yorkshire, bequeathed his property for the
establishment of a school, which was opened in 1787 and affords free
education to fifty children. (York Trust Property Books.)

[44] The following list of schools is of interest:

School	Founded	Capacity	School	Founded	Capacity
Sidcot	1808	133	Ayton	1841	105
Wigton	1815	68	Sibford	1842	83
Rawdon	1832	70	Bootham	1823	85
Penketh	1834	80	The Mount	1831	83

The first six of these are coeducational; Bootham is for boys; The
Mount is for girls.

(the Friends' Educational Society) with various committees of women, by means of which the teachers were to be enabled to effect an exchange of practical experience and to obtain a general view of the results of the different educational methods. The annual reports of this Society, which engages in historical research in addition to its other work, contain much valuable information.

In any comprehensive view of the educational activities of the Quakers, one point stands out clear: the sense of obligation of the meeting to provide all children with education. This feeling of obligation is noteworthy primarily in that it was recognized long before the time at which children were officially counted as members. The suggestions of Fox, Penn, and others that there should be complete spiritual and manual training were never entirely realized, owing to the lack of means and of general interest. Yet the effort to foster spiritual development proved vital enough, in spite of Bellers's propaganda, to prevent the exclusive attention to manual skill. The Quakers deliberately refused to exploit the children for their labor, although down to the beginning of the nineteenth century such exploitation was not only popularly justified but actually advocated;[45] and by this refusal they placed themselves far in advance of their contemporaries.

The zeal for the improvement of the schools developed only slowly; but it must be noted that whatever was accomplished was for the benefit of all children, whether rich or poor. The ancient principle was adhered to, that

[45] See, for instance, Defoe and Richardson, *A Tour through the Island of Great Britain,* 8th edition London 1778, iii, 155ff., where the authors speak with approval of the fact that in the cloth factories in Yorkshire children only four years old were prepared to earn their living.

the possibilities of spiritual development in each child should determine the kind of education he received, not the accident of his birth; direct financial assistance from the meeting is replaced by a policy of tuition charges graded according to the means of the parents, with no resulting distinction in the treatment accorded the children.

A striking innovation was the acceptance of children whose parents had only an indirect connection with Quakers, or none at all; although, as may be easily understood, the children of members received the preference, since contributions from the meetings formed the principal source of support of the schools. There were funds available in most meetings intended to be used for higher education along scientific or technical lines, and also to assist needy young people to set themselves up in business or to purchase equipment when entering a special line of employment; and all scholars of their schools, whether they were boys or girls, whether they were members or nonmembers, had the same claim to assistance from these funds.

The significance of the Quaker schools for the training of the younger generation of the Society has not been so great during the last few decades. For the excellent board schools ⁴⁰ and middle-class high schools now make it appear that special sacrifices on the part of the Quaker meetings are hardly necessary. The early scruples of the Quakers about sending their children to these schools have been largely removed by the fact that religious instruction in these schools, in accordance with the

⁴⁰ In England, a school under the control of a school board.

requirement of the law, is on a broad Christian basis,
but is nonsectarian, and discussion is not permitted of matters of faith in which the individual sects differ from each
other.[47]

According to a statistical estimate for the year 1909,
there were 1657 children (1489 boarders and 168 day
scholars) in the fifteen schools maintained by the meetings of England and Ireland; of these pupils only 55 per
cent were members of the Society.[48] Many of the children
of Quakers are now educated in other schools and to
some extent they thus may get out of touch with Quakerism. Some of the external marks of Quakerism in the
matter of "speech, behavior, and apparel" have been
given up in recent years, for reasons which may be readily
understood; and the maintenance of their religious principles has unquestionably been endangered by this course.
It seems therefore desirable that the Society should again
get under the burden of the careful education of its children.[49]

The efforts of the Quakers in the interest of education
as so far considered contributed, with few exceptions,
essentially to the advantage of their own members; but
over and above these activities Friends have labored con-

[47] Here too a direct Quaker influence may be assumed; for the Education Bill of 1870, which provided for universal compulsory education
and also regulated religious instruction in the schools, is the work of
William Edward Forster (1818-1886), who was born a Quaker. See the
biography of Forster by T. Wemyss Reid, London 1888.
[48] Yearly Meeting Minutes for 1910.
[49] This concern has been expressed by some of the leading members
of the Society, such as Joseph Rowntree and Edward Grubb; and also in
a report which was sent by the meeting of Overseers to the Yearly Meeting in 1910, and was reprinted in the Minutes.

tinuously, and on a large scale, for popular education and training. This activity does not begin until toward the end of the eighteenth century, at the period when, as we saw above, the economic condition of the Society was so well assured that there was energy available for general humanitarian purposes, and when at the same time the discovery of gross abuses offered a commanding challenge to a wide circle of people for constructive assistance.

Even Adam Smith and Malthus, in their principal works, refer to the necessity of popular education. Instead of the so-called charity schools, which did not nearly suffice to supply the demand, Smith wants to establish public schools in each parish, "where children may be taught for a reward so moderate, that even a common labourer may afford it." [50] By requiring that children should pass an examination before being accepted as apprentices in a trade, pressure could be brought to bear on them to attend school. Smith shows also the advantages to the state of a better school education; but the government, for decades thereafter, did not even take steps to encourage private initiative in establishing schools. [51]

In 1803 Malthus writes: "It is surely a great national disgrace, that the education of the lower classes of people in England should be left merely to a few Sunday schools,

[50] Adam Smith, *Wealth of Nations,* edited by E. Cannan, London and New York 1904, bk. v, ch. i, p. 270. Smith fears that the teachers, if paid exclusively from public funds, will be lax in the performance of their office.

[51] In 1833 the first governmental subventions were granted to the British and Foreign School Society and to the National Society for the Education of Children, founded in 1808 and 1811 respectively.

supported by a subscription from individuals, who, of course, can give to the course of instruction in them any kind of bias which they please." [52] He absolutely rejects the idea that popular education is to be feared as entirely unjustified, and holds up Scotland as proof that a rebellious and discontented spirit is not awakened by learning.

In *The Philanthropist,* a publication edited by the Quaker William Allen, the number of children in England and Wales at the beginning of the nineteenth century is estimated at 2,000,000. The children in London alone are estimated at 50,000, of whom more than half "grow up to an adult state, without any instruction at all, in the grossest ignorance, and without any useful impression of religion or morality." [53] This universal neglect of education, however, filled the penal institutions with criminals.

Three different kinds of organization were set up by the Quakers for the advancement of popular education: the Sunday Schools (which were primarily designed for children), the Adult Schools, and the Lancaster Schools. We will consider first the Lancaster Schools, since these, in contrast with the other two types of institution, have a long history behind them.

Joseph Lancaster, born in Southwark in 1778 of a godly Quaker family, had served as assistant in his youth in a boarding school and in a day school, and thus had had abundant opportunity to become acquainted with the defi-

[52] T. R. Malthus, *An Essay on the Principle of Population . . .,* Georgetown 1809 (1st American edition, from the 3d London edition), ii, 413 (vol. 2, bk. 4, ch. 8).
[53] *The Philanthropist,* i, 8off.

ciencies of the ancient system of education.[54] These deficiencies, and the wretched plight of many poor children,
especially in the parish workhouses, who never had the
advantage of any sort of education, impelled him to take
active steps on his own account. When he was only eight-
een years old, he opened a primitive kind of school in
a shed which his father placed at his disposal, in which he
soon assembled ninety children about him—a number
which increased rapidly when he was able to rent larger
quarters. On the outside of his schoolroom he posted a
notice of the following import: "All who will, may send
their children, and have them educated, Freely (the ex-
pence of Writing Books excepted); and those to whom
the above Offer may not prove acceptable, may pay for
them at a very moderate Price." [55] This liberality was
made possible by an especially inexpensive system of
instruction, which soon received Lancaster's name, although it is not to be thought of exactly as original with
him.[56]

The essential element of the new method of teaching
was that a number of boys were trained up to be helpers
of the teacher (so-called "monitors"), and assumed as
their principal task the guidance of the other pupils, in
accordance with Lancaster's principles: "The teacher
should be only a silent spectator and overseer. The less

[54] In the introduction to his essay, *Improvements in Education as it
Respects the Industrious Classes,* London 1803 (3d edition 1805), Lancaster gave a detailed exposition of these deficiencies.

[55] *Improvements,* etc., p. 25.

[56] He himself admits in his writings (*Improvements,* etc., pp. 46, 47, 60)
that he is indebted to Dr. Andrew Bell's experiment in education in the
men's asylum at Madras, India, for many valuable suggestions. Dr.
Bell (1753-1832) had founded there a system of education similar to the
one which he used.

EDUCATION

the pupils hear the voice of the teacher, the better they
will obey him. The disturbance in a school is usually proportional to the noise that the teacher himself makes;
punishment of the pupils and exhaustion of the teacher
are interdependent." All the pupils of a school—and
there were often as many as a thousand—were assembled
in one room; but they were divided into little classes, with
a monitor at the head of each one, who was responsible
for the progress of his group in their studies, and for their
orderliness, neatness, and good behavior, and who made
a report every day. In the instruction, the chief emphasis
was laid on the principle that all children should be kept
occupied so that they would be obliged to concentrate
their attention. For instance, if the teacher read out
single words, the children spelled them and wrote them
down, and the monitor managed their slates or sand
boxes, for writing was often done with the finger in dry
sand. A similar method was followed in teaching reading and arithmetic. A whole system of rewards was
devised for its effect in stimulating interest; the helpers,
in addition, received one penny a day for their trouble.
The other expenses were very slight—pupils did not
have their own books; so that in a school of 300
pupils a payment of seven shillings a year for each
child was enough; and with a larger number the
expense and consequently the price was correspondingly
lower.

However primitive this method of teaching appears to
us now, at the beginning of the nineteenth century it had
very great value. William Allen, for instance, writes that
he was absolutely astounded at his first visit to a Lan-

caster School: [57] "Here I beheld a thousand children collected from the streets, where they were learning nothing
but mischief, one bad boy corrupting another, all reduced
to the most perfect order, training to habits of subordina-
tion and usefulness, and learning the great truths of the
gospel from the Bible." [58]

Approval by the King of this system, and regular yearly
contributions from the highest nobility, [59] by which wider
circles were spurred on to contribute, made it possible for
Lancaster to set up numerous schools throughout the
country. Moreover, funds were placed at his disposal in
such sums that for most of the pupils he was almost immediately able to do away with the small charge for tuition
with which he had started. Especially needy children
were even fed, for Lancaster was concerned to improve
the lot of poor children in every possible way. [60]

Lancaster's plans were laid on a grand scale, but as a
business organizer he proved to be inadequate to the task
of extending his school system, and he got into debt. The
undertaking was only saved by a group of persons, mainly
from Quaker circles, who organized in 1808 as trustees

[57] See James Sherman, *Memoir of William Allen,* Philadelphia
[1851], p. 60.

[58] The text of the Bible was used as the basis of instruction in reading and writing, though there was no discussion of the various interpre-
tations put upon the text by different sects. This practice occasionally
brought upon Lancaster, as upon the Quakers as a sect, the reproach of
deism, but did not cause any diminution of interest in the pedagogical
method, nor interfere with public appreciation of its value.

[59] There was formed a "Committee for promoting the Royal Lancastrian System for the Education of the Poor," at the head of which were
the Duke of Bedford and Lord Somerville.

[60] In a letter to John Foster (1740-1828), Chancellor of the Exchequer
in Ireland in 1805, he again agitates the question of combining instruction and industrial work, and suggests various occupations which would
be profitable in Ireland.

and assumed the responsibility for the finances. The annual reports of this committee afford us a picture of the extensive development of the so-called Royal Lancastrian System of Education. In 1812 it is stated that, though no accurate count had been made, it was safe to assume, from the number of books bought, that several hundred of the Lancaster schools were in operation.[61] More than half of the pupils at this time belonged to the Established Church, and the religious instruction therefore was under the direction of the clergy.

In 1813 Lancaster, who hitherto had accepted no personal remuneration for his labors, found it advisable to establish a private school, in order that he might have some income for his own family. In order to assure the complete separation of this school from his public undertakings, the Society insisted that Lancaster should no longer be a member of the managing committee, which continued its work under the name British and Foreign School Society.[62] As early as 1814 Lancaster's school, upon which he had set great hopes, became bankrupt, and this brought about his disownment from the Society of Friends. He perhaps received some consolation from the fact that, in spite of his expulsion, it was made possible

[61] Lancaster engaged in propaganda for his plan on many lecture tours throughout England and Scotland; in 1810 he is said to have delivered sixty-seven public addresses, the result of which was the establishment of fifty schools with 14,000 to 15,000 pupils. Such schools were projected also for Africa, North and South America, and India. The annual income in 1810 amounted to about £1000. In spite of this income there was a considerable deficit, but there were always persons to be found who would advance money on credit. In 1810, for instance, Robert Owen is listed among the creditors in the amount of £250.

[62] Its aim was "to afford education, procure employment, and, so far as possible, to furnish clothing to the children of the poorer subjects of King George III."

for him to emigrate to America a few years later, through the action of a number of Quakers, his former fellow believers, who gave him financial assistance; and that in North and South America his efforts to extend his school system were crowned with great success.

The activity of the British and Foreign School Society, which, like the National Society for the Education of the Poor, received subventions from the government and was thus able to do much toward establishing better schools, cannot be pursued any further in this discussion, since our present task is only to record the part played by the Quakers in popular education.

Passing now to the Sunday School, which, like the Lancastrian school, was designed primarily for children, we can make our discussion much briefer; and at the start we may note that in this field of work the Quakers were not pioneers. In 1785 a large group of philanthropically inclined persons had formed themselves into an association called the Sunday School Society, the purpose of which was to provide some sort of instruction, on Sunday at least, for children who were employed all the rest of the week. The Sunday Schools were intended primarily for children employed in the factories, but other children were admitted [63] also. Instruction was provided by unpaid volunteers, and the Sunday School Society supplied the books. From about 1800 the Quakers followed this same plan; in the course of years the instruction took on a predominantly religious character, free, in accordance

[63] Sir Frederick Morton Eden draws attention (*The State of the Poor*, London 1797, i, 428) to the fact that, at the end of the eighteenth century schooling cost so much that many persons even in the middle classes could not provide the amount charged.

EDUCATION

with Quaker principles, of all denominational spirit and
not at all directed toward making proselytes. At the end
of 1909 the Quakers were maintaining 240 such schools,
with about 28,000 pupils and teachers, whereas the total
membership of the Society in England was not quite
18,000.

There was need for instruction, however, not only on
the part of children, but of adults. After the children had
acquired an elementary education, parents felt their own
lack of schooling with increased poignancy. In contrast
to the situation in Wales, where persons from six to sev-
enty years of age attended the so-called circulating
schools, it was not customary for adults to be enrolled in
the Sunday Schools; and, as larger and larger groups from
the working classes withdrew from the church, many
people were entirely without religious contacts.

The credit for pioneer work in evolving a way to combat this sad situation belongs to William Singleton, a
Methodist. In 1798 he established a course of instruction for adults in Nottingham; the Quaker Samuel Fox
assisted him in this project, and later assumed the management of it. Quakers in other cities followed suit with
similar institutions, and thus from these modest beginnings there developed the Adult Schools, which have been
of great benefit over a wide range. In their own statutes
they are now officially designated as "fellowships" of men
and women for study and worship, formed especially "for
the purpose of mutual helpfulness." [64] The inclusion of

[64] *Adult Schools, their Aims and Methods,* issued by the National
Council 1902. See also Edgar F. Hobley and Thomas W. Mercer, *The
Adult School Movement, What it is and What it may Become,* London
[1910]; G. Currie Martin, *The Adult School Movement,* London 1924.

women corresponds to the Quaker principle of complete equality between the sexes; but it is especially worthy of note that the first courses of instruction of this kind were set up for women exclusively—for the women operatives in the lace and stocking factories of Nottingham. Dr. Pole,[65] in his book about these courses, brings out the necessity of education for women, because of their very great influence, not only upon growing children but upon their husbands; for the latter could be kept out of the alehouses if the wives provided comfortable home surroundings. Dr. Pole sees in this influence the possibility for the laboring classes of improvement in their economic status.

Parallel with the women's classes there soon were established classes for men and for young people. The latter were considered as a continuation of the Sunday School, which carried the children along only far enough to let them go without oversight at the very age at which they are most exposed to temptations.

The subjects of instruction in the Adult Schools were at first only reading from the Bible, and writing; also, for those who had made some little progress, arithmetic. Meetings for worship were not started until later; there was no attempt to proselytize nor was membership in any denomination made a condition of admission to an Adult School. "The only qualification for membership is a wish to join the school. The members of a school may belong to any denomination or none." [66]

In the course of decades, after elementary instruction

[65] Thomas Pole, *A History of the Origin and Progress of Adult Schools,* Bristol 1814.

[66] John Wilhelm Rowntree and Henry Bryan Binns, *A History of the Adult School Movement,* London 1903.

had become general, the basis of Adult School instruction was changed. The emphasis came to be laid upon moral education, as this, after the former gross ignorance had in a measure been relieved, seemed the most obvious need. Nowadays the Adult Schools might be designated as discussion groups or forums. Between the leader [67] and the rest of the group there exists a friendly spirit of comradeship; discussion offers everybody a chance for free expression; and the members take part as much as possible in the administration of school affairs.

In connection with the Adult Schools there arose various other institutions for the benefit of the members, as for instance health insurance and savings funds. The latter, however, through the introduction by the government of the postal savings system, have become less important, as the members were encouraged from this time to deposit their savings in the government system. The courses of instruction have proved very effective for the dissemination of the temperance movement, directly through propaganda and indirectly through the establishment of libraries and the encouragement of a higher type of social life than was offered in the public house.

The success of the Quakers was not only sufficient to arouse the interest of wide circles of persons outside the limits of the Society; but it even stirred them to activity along the same lines—though, to be sure, this came only after some decades of activity on the part of the Quakers. Naturally, these courses founded independently of the Quaker Adult Schools were for the time being isolated,

[67] The teaching is done without pay, by men and women of many different occupations.

and therefore much weaker than the schools of the Friends, which had the support of the central organization.[68] And it is a beautiful example of the way in which the Quakers put public interest above that of their own Society,[69] that they gave up the advantages of exclusiveness in order to make possible a union of all the Adult Schools. Prominent leaders of such Quaker schools opened the way for an amalgamation of all the schools of single districts (the Adult School Unions) from 1884 on, and, as a central organization, formed the National Council of Adult School Unions in 1889, composed of twenty-four members, of whom more than half are Quakers.

As the situation now stands,[70] the Adult School seems destined to be the church of the future for the working classes.

[68] They were placed under the care of the Friends' First Day School Association, founded in 1847.

[69] This point of view is expressed in the first annual conference of the National Council of Adult School Unions.

[70] According to census reports at the beginning of the twentieth century, only one seventh of the population attended any sort of church service.

CHAPTER THREE

THE BATTLE AGAINST ALCOHOLISM

JUST as the Quakers from the very beginning struggled against poverty and ignorance as hindrances to the efforts of men to raise themselves to a higher level of religious and moral life, so also they directed their energies against another of the great causes of social and spiritual distress —alcoholism. It might appear, to be sure, that the earliest Friends paid little attention to the dangers of indulgence in alcohol—even in the workhouse at Clerkenwell,[1] according to early accounts of the care given to inmates, "sufficient beer" was allowed as a part of each ration. Moreover, beer and wine were served in connection with the business meetings (the monthly, quarterly, and yearly meetings), at which nowadays tea plays an important part. This care can be explained, however, by the general attitude of the time, which looked upon spirituous liquors of some kind, or even the stronger alcoholic drinks, as necessary to health, and considered the ordinary consumption of wine and beer as a matter of course, attended by no harmful result.

Excessive drinking, on the contrary, was early condemned by the Quakers. Thus Fox relates that the senseless habit of pledging him with toasts was one of the

[1] See above, p. 83 (note).

causes that led him in 1643 to cut himself off from his relatives.[2] In an address to the Protector and Parliament,[3] of the year 1658, Fox makes the demand—and he feels himself commissioned by God himself to urge this matter upon the attention of the ruling authorities—that licenses to do business as brewers or innkeepers should be granted exclusively to dependable, god-fearing people,[4] who should lodge travelers and dispense beer only to persons who were not able to brew beer for their own use. "The multitude of other inns all over the country, which are not equipped to lodge anybody, serve only to seduce the young people to frivolity and folly, and ruin the divine creation; for through drinking come sinful thoughts, and the temptation to steal, in order to get more money to satisfy the evil desires. By this means the world is debauched, and men are brought into contempt." In an address of 1659,[5] Fox voices further earnest warnings against entrusting any public office to a drunkard.

Both these admonitions fell in an evil time. The Institute of Major-Generals,[6] which had been founded by Cromwell with the function of policing public morals outside London, and was expected to raise the general level of morality by closing all the alehouses, had given way

[2] Journal, i, 3.

[3] To the Protector and Parliament of England, printed for Giles Calvert 1658, p. 11.

[4] Licenses for alehouses were introduced under James I; the sale of alcoholic beverages continued free in Scotland and Ireland.

[5] To the Parliament of the Commonwealth of England, printed for Thomas Simmons 1659, pp. 7, 8.

[6] See S. R. Gardiner, History of the Commonwealth and Protectorate 1649-1660, 3 vols., 3d edition London 1901, iii, 172ff., 236. See also Wolfgang Michael, Cromwell, 2 vols., 1907, ii, 86.

THE BATTLE AGAINST ALCOHOLISM

before the popular discontent.[7] Down to the time of the
Restoration drunkenness increased so much that even
Charles II, who in most matters can hardly be called puritanical, expressed displeasure in his very first proclamation at the eternal wasting of time in alehouses, and at
those of his subjects "who expressed their devotion to
their king in no other way than by drinking his health."[8]
Strict enforcement of the laws against drunkenness was
now required of all police officials; but in spite of that,
there must have been[9] a considerable increase in the consumption of alcohol,[10] as shown by the increased importation of French wine and brandy. The harm resulting to
public morals and health, and, by no means least, to the
economic situation, led in 1678 to the absolute prohibition
of the importation of spirituous liquors, and when this
proved impracticable, to a high import tariff. With the
institution of this policy the English awoke to the fact
that the only way to control the misuse of alcohol is to
make it difficult to procure, since it is useless to count
upon voluntary moderation.

[7] It was abolished in 1657.
[8] These conditions obtained however only in the south; in the north
the consumption of alcohol was considerably less, in accordance with
the general eating habits observed there. Vegetables, potatoes, and por-
ridge formed the staple articles of diet for the middle classes in the
north, whereas in southern England—presumably because of the higher
costs of fuel—relatively few foods were consumed which needed cooking.
The poorest classes lived almost exclusively on bread, cheese, and tea,
and allowed themselves, in comparison with their small incomes, very
considerable quantities of alcohol. See Frederick Morton Eden, *The State
of the Poor,* 3 vols., London 1797, i, 542.
[9] See W. A. S. Hewins, *English Trade and Finance . . .,* London
1892, pp. 134, 135.
[10] On the enormous increase in the consumption of beer which occurred
at the same time, see Faber, *Die Entstehung des Agrarschutzes in England* (The rise of agrarian protection in England), Strassburg 1888,
pp. 20, 21.

The Quakers, to be sure, expected this self-control from the members of their faith. Again and again the annual epistles [11] admonish Friends to be moderate in their use of intoxicating beverages; they are especially urged to accustom their children to simplicity and moderation, so that they may be preserved later from danger. It is considered the duty of every member of the Society to lead a temperate life, in order to avoid all occasion of possible reproach against Quakerism. The regulating function of the monthly meetings which had existed with regard to such matters was made more definite in 1755, when a query regarding the use of alcohol was added to those which were to be answered to the Yearly Meeting. If any member, in spite of these admonitions, brought disgrace upon the Society through drunkenness, he was disowned; even as early as 1678 we hear of disciplinary action for this cause,[12] and a summary of the cases of disownment [13] by the London Quarterly Meeting between 1735 and 1794 shows that "disorderly conduct, drinking, gaming, etc.," as a cause stood second in order of frequency.[14]

In Pennsylvania, where the Quakers at first had a free hand in the regulation of all social relationships, it was easier for them to give effect to their zeal for temperance than in England. It is characteristic of Penn's attitude for him to have laid down as a fundamental principle

[11] For instance, see Yearly Meeting Epistles of 1691, 1751, 1754, 1834, etc.

[12] Beck and Ball, p. 317.

[13] Beck and Ball, p. 123.

[14] The most frequent cause of disownment has always been, until recently, marriage performed by a clergyman or marriage to a non-member.

that no saloons or alehouses should be tolerated—a requirement which was modified in the final charter of Pennsylvania to the extent that article vii made the granting of licenses for the sale of liquor conditional upon the recommendation of a judge, and permitted the revocation of the license of any public house that proved to be disorderly.[15] In Penn's view, "To wink at a trade that effeminates the people, and invades the ancient discipline of the kingdom, is a crime capital, and to be severely punished instead of being excused by the magistrate." [16] Penn, as a natural consequence, would have nothing whatever to do with the popular practice of outwitting the natives by making them drunk, and declined very advantageous offers for the monopoly of trade with the Indians, for the reason that he wished to protect the aborigines from being debauched by alcohol. As spirituous liquors enjoyed free entry, however, the repeated injunction of the Philadelphia Yearly Meeting not to sell alcoholic beverages to the Indians, nor to give them in exchange for other goods, could not be enforced. Even during his lifetime Penn, in a letter to the Free Society of Traders, lamented the thirst of the Indians for alcohol, and after his death the sale of rum to the natives increased to such an extent that an investigation of the condition of the Indians, brought about at the instance of the New York Yearly Meeting, determined that the misuse of spirituous liquors was the

[15] See *Minutes of the Provincial Council of Pennsylvania,* Philadelphia 1852, ii, 59.

[16] Frederick Sessions, *Two and a half Centuries of Temperance Work in the Society of Friends, 1643-1893,* a lecture delivered in February 1893, p. 9. Sessions quotes Penn's *Some Fruits of Solitude in Reflections and Maxims* (originally published London 1693; see edition by John Clifford, London 1905, p. 152), part 2, § 231.

principal cause of their misery, and the chief obstacle
to the advance of civilization.[17]

In England, too, the Quakers did not limit their temperance activities to the circle of their Society. They
hoped, specifically, to bring about a general improvement
through a strengthening of the feeling of responsibility
on the part of the alehouse keepers. Thus George Whitehead writes:[18] "You who keep alehouses, take thought
in the fear of God, the righteous Judge, that you may
perform your office so as to keep your consciences clear
in the eyes of God and man. Do not make your living
from the sins of the people; do not let your profits flow
from this source. Be careful not to offer to any man or
woman more strong liquor than is necessary to their refreshment or their health. Remember the sad consequences of excess, of drunkenness, what they are and
whither they lead." This warning was called forth again,
a hundred years later, when the Quaker James Wood
said:[19] "It is one of the greatest commandments that
we should love our neighbor as ourselves; but how do we
observe this commandment if we see him drunken and
offer him additional spirituous liquor for immediate use,
so that his health is injured, his family rendered unhappy,
and, what is worse, his soul kept in a condition of darkness, and he himself becomes entirely incapable of enjoying heavenly things—the only true good, for which he

[17] *A Summary Account of the Measures pursued by the Yearly Meeting of Friends of New York for the Welfare and Civilization of the
Indians . . .*, London 1813.
[18] George Whitehead, *The Cause and Prevention of Great Calamities
national and personal, demonstrated . . .*, 1692.
[19] James Wood, *To Inn-Keepers, Ale-House Keepers, and all others
whom it may concern*, 1796.

was created. . . . We shall have to render an account on the Day of Judgment. Public houses do not exist for the purpose of reveling, but for refreshment and for the accommodation of strangers. Let me earnestly admonish every single one of you to ask yourselves, when you hand liquor to others: 'Am I acting toward these people as I should honestly wish that they should act toward me and mine? Am I taking pains, in so far as I am able, to keep a conscience void of offense toward God and man?' "

Even at that time the idea was gaining ground that it was reprehensible not only to use or serve intoxicating liquors to excess, but even to manufacture them. Such manufacture was considered an injustice to the poor, inasmuch as the use of grains for distilling and beer making raised the price of bread; but it was felt that it was an even greater sin for men to take what God bestowed for the maintenance of life and change it into beverages which destroy life.[20]

The conviction that for Quakers themselves it would be better to have nothing at all to do with the business of brewing or dispensing liquor is of very early date. In records of the Quakers in Devonshire for September 29, 1705, the minute occurs: "James Goodridge to be advised to give up the retailing of brandy and strong liquors in his house at the bridge, as it does tend to the dishonour of truth" (i.e., the Quaker faith).[21] Quakers voluntarily gave up the manufacture and sale of alcoholic beverages

[20] Anthony Benezet, *Serious Considerations on several important Subjects . . . and remarks on the nature and bad effects of Spirituous Liquors,* Philadelphia, printed by Joseph Crukshank 1778.
[21] Quoted by Samuel Bowly, in *The Sale and Use of Intoxicating Liquors,* in *Friends' Quarterly Examiner,* vol. vi (1872), p. 381.

during the following decades, though not in any striking number until the beginning of the nineteenth century,[22] in spite of the fact that they thus deprived themselves of sources of income which were often quite lucrative; and men whose previous environment gave them the soundest judgment on the question of intemperance often became pioneers in temperance work.

This applies especially to Thomas Shillitoe (1754-1836),[23] who, born in an innkeeper's family, exhibited unwavering zeal, a quarter of a century before the formation of the temperance unions, in rooting out the evils of drunkenness. Thomas Shillitoe is one of the most important philanthropists among the Quakers, though but little known. After he had acquired the means to enable him to live from his income (he had a position at first in a bank, but later chose to follow the humbler calling of shoemaker), he felt it to be his duty to devote himself at home and abroad to the service of God and the church. He labored for prison reform and for the abolition of slavery; and in addition he worked to overcome all the hindrances to religious progress, which appeared to him to be particularly threatened by the misuse of alcohol. Just as the early Quakers had railed in the churches against the evil practices of the clergy, and had thus brought upon themselves the wrath of the people, so Shillitoe preached temperance in the alehouses in spite of curses and actual violence. These discouragements did not deter him from making even more exacting demands,

[22] Nevertheless, there are admonitions to do so in the Yearly Meeting minutes as late as 1835.

[23] See William Tallack, *Thomas Shillitoe, the Quaker Missionary and Temperance Pioneer*, London 1867.

by advocating total abstinence instead of moderation, after he had found out by experiment upon himself that this not only did him no harm, but was actually beneficial to his health.

With the promulgation of this point of view the movement enters upon a new phase, and becomes really effective. Exhortations to "temperance" (i.e., moderation) could be interpreted in any way that might be convenient; and, even though Penn had emphasized the fact that "the smaller the drink, the clearer the head and the cooler the blood," and would not admit the usefulness of strong spirituous liquors except as medicine, this point of view found but little acceptance even among his brothers in the faith.[24] Not until the nineteenth century did the agitation have any lasting effect. Quakers led the way by abolishing alcohol from various private enterprises. Allen, for instance, reports of Lindfield: "Beer is not allowed in the colony. At the time of its establishment drunkenness was very common, but now it is extraordinarily rare, nor are there any more cases of theft."

Proof was brought forward that even hard physical labor could be performed without the use of stimulants, and that alcohol was absolutely lacking in food content. The Quaker physician John Fothergill (1784-1858) of Darlington (to be distinguished from the earlier and more famous Dr. John Fothergill of London) then established the positively harmful effects of alcohol, and thus took the last step in the development of the theory of total abstinence. At about the same time a group of Quakers

[24] W. Penn, *Some Fruits of Solitude in Reflections and Maxims,* part 1, §§ 65-67 (Clifford's edition, p. 37).

sent an invitation to the whole membership in the Society, along with an essay by Edward Smith, of Sheffield, in which it was shown that the *regular* use of spirituous liquors, not merely excessive indulgence, was the cause of poverty, sickness, and irreligion. The point was further made that drinking does not ordinarily stop at the consumption of small quantities: "the intention to be moderate is daily found to be of no avail against the constant temptation resulting from inclination and public custom."[25]

The Yearly Meeting as a body did not lag behind its individual members in zeal. In 1830 it appointed a large number of persons to visit all the meetings and report on the temperance question; and in 1835 there followed the official admonition to total abstinence. Those who are strong enough to be safe from being led into excesses are urged to pledge themselves to self-restraint as a good example to others who may be weaker.[26] The first result was an extension of temperance agitation, which had gotten under way in America on a large scale. In 1826, the American Temperance Society had been founded in Boston, as a result of the discovery that two-thirds of the pauperism, nine-tenths of the crime, and two-thirds of all cases of mental disease could be traced directly or indirectly to the use of alcohol. Following the example of America, a union of societies was effected in London in 1836, resulting in the British and Foreign Temperance Society. This association does not consist exclusively of

[25] "Be it remembered that he who takes intoxicating liquors in moderation walks at the edge of a precipice and is constantly on the point of falling."

[26] The *Discipline* also says (p. 109): "It is alike the duty and the privilege of the Christian to deny himself for the sake of the fallen or the weak."

Quakers, but its leading men have generally been members of the Society; in London the meetings were held in the Quaker headquarters, and branches were formed there.[27] In 1839 the pledge of moderation was changed to a pledge of total abstinence, as the Quakers had been recommending for years. Renewed propaganda work for total abstinence was engaged in by many, including especially the Quaker Joseph Eaton with his *Address to the Society of Friends on the Temperance Reformation* (London 1839), in which he lays special emphasis on utilizing to a better purpose the money which had hitherto been expended on spirituous liquors.

As soon as the Quakers became aware that alcohol had no value as a food, but had actually a harmful effect, and also that not only spirituous liquors should be given up, but beer as well, they abolished, in 1843, the use of alcoholic beverages of any kind at all their public functions and at social gatherings. According to Sessions the credit for this final victory of the total abstainers belongs to the Friends of Yorkshire, who converted to their way of thinking the Quakers who up till then had approved the system of licensing. Concessions to sell liquor were now abolished on the so-called Quaker railroad, the Stockton-Darlington line.

The Friends' Temperance Union now carries on the fight against alcohol outside the Society, but works in conjunction with other organizations, as for instance, the Adult Schools. Just as formerly the laborer was kept away from the alehouse through teaching and entertainment, so an effort is now made at the lunch hours and

[27] Called Temperance Provident Associations.

other free times to break the hold of alcohol by serving coffee. The various welfare organizations founded by Quaker employers all have the same purpose—to moderate or if possible to abolish altogether the indulgence in alcohol. Thus, for instance, in the colony at Bournville, the predominant wish of the founder, George Cadbury, was to offer to those who settled there employment and diversion during the evenings through garden work, in place of the "recreation" in the alehouse which was usual elsewhere.

The members of the Society itself have given no cause, for a long time, for further agitation against alcohol. To be sure, it is not yet true that total abstinence is required of members—even the special association of Quakers who were total abstainers, founded in 1852, did not win over all the membership to its point of view; but the Society is getting closer and closer to this goal, and will probably, without forcing the issue, attain it in the near future.

CHAPTER FOUR

PUBLIC HEALTH; CARE OF THE INSANE

I. PUBLIC HEALTH

ALTHOUGH the care exercised by the Quakers in behalf of the sick has been already briefly mentioned in connection with their efforts toward the relief of all kinds of distress, nevertheless a more detailed treatment should be accorded to their ideas and accomplishments with respect to sickness as a social problem. We have already referred to the services rendered by Quaker women to the sick and distressed, and spoken of the liberal extension of help to cases of sickness among the poor that were outside their membership. Their idea has also been touched upon that the state should feel a duty in the matter of the support of the helpless: in the addresses of Fox [1] and others of the early Quakers we find constant emphasis upon the duty of the community toward the blind, the lame, and the crippled.

For under an economic system which imposed considerable hardship on the entire lower class, these unfortunates were the ones who suffered most. At the same time that the economic upheaval had deprived hosts of the

---

[1] For instance, *A Warning to all the Merchants in London . . .*, London 1658, and *To the Protector and Parliament of England*, London 1659.

rural population and of the industrial workers in the cities of their main support in time of need, the charitable help of the church had been considerably diminished as a result of the Reformation. With the distribution of the property of the monasteries to the favorites of Henry VIII, one of the most important sources of help for the sick was cut off. To be sure, a few new hospitals were built and endowed by the crown, and there were still private institutions for the benefit of those in need; but givers became less liberal when the idea of providing for the salvation of their souls ceased to have force as a motive to liberality.[2]

Aside from the difficulty arising from the insufficiency of financial support, the charitably inclined—and this applies to poor as well as rich—lacked trained knowledge as to how to treat cases of sickness. The almsgivers in the monasteries had been able to gain a certain degree of practical experience in the care of the sick, and had thus made medical service more or less available to the masses —for even from the large hospitals very little such service was dispensed. After the Reformation such efforts were limited to the distribution of household necessities or of strengthening food to sick persons who were too poor to buy their own—for the sick remained for the most part in their own homes.

The idea of special diet for the sick was as yet unknown. Even the first Quakers did no more, so far as can be definitely ascertained, than meet the exigencies of physical need and offer religious consolation. The miraculous

[2] On the efficacy of this motive see Gerhard Uhlhorn, *Christian Charity in the Ancient Church,* New York 1883, p. 293ff.: a translation of vol. 1 of his *Die Christliche Liebesthätigkeit in der alten Kirche,* 1st edition Stuttgart 1882.

cures that Fox tells about [3]—they agree very closely with those recorded in the Bible—cannot be clearly judged; they have nothing in common with the systematic care of the sick. There is even a certain amount of contempt of medical skill to be felt—prayer and the laying on of hands prove effective, where the doctors fail. But this too is not surprising. Of what significance was the science of the world in comparison with the power of faith! However, systematic medicine was still in its infancy; so that it is easy to understand that the Quakers of the seventeenth century, among whom there were few physicians, had very little respect for it.

The necessity of improving and perfecting the science of medical care was first agitated by Bellers. His *Essay towards the Improvement of Physick* [4] brings the humanitarian appeal of improved medical knowledge into relation with its practical usefulness to science, and hence with the self-interest of the wealthy, and therefore dominant, classes.

First in importance, in Bellers's plan, is the establishment of hospitals for the poor. Exact records are to be kept of all cases of sickness which occur there. The dead are to be dissected for the instruction of the physicians. The physicians in their turn are to avail themselves of this advantage as much as possible; those not connected with

---

[3] For instance, *Journal,* i, 46, 133, 258; ii, 176, 192, 377. In Fox's journal as he wrote it the instances are even more numerous and striking, since the miracles constitute a feature which the editor was inclined to omit. See A. Neave Brayshaw, *The Personality of George Fox,* London 1919, Appendix B.

[4] *Essay towards the Improvement of Physick. In twelve Proposals. By which the Lives of Many Thousands of the Rich as well as of the Poor may be Saved Yearly.* Humbly dedicated to the Parliament of Great Britain by John Bellers, London 1714.

any hospital are to have access to the dissections, so that residence abroad, which had hitherto been essential to the pursuit of medical studies, may no longer be necessary.

This proposal (proposal i) is similar to another (vi), which suggests the establishment of university clinics; for "the combination of practice with theory is an absolute necessity for the better kind of training." Hitherto it had not been easy for the students to secure a corpse for dissection, because the masses felt outraged by the practice, and would not allow it. Bellers recommends that the cases in the university clinics should be distributed according to the different diseases; and in the same way he proposes (iii) that separate hospitals be established for each specific kind of sickness or defect, so that, for instance, there would be a special institution for the blind. Those who are pronounced incurable are also to be cared for in special houses; physicians must have opportunity to attempt cures for such cases, the success to be rewarded by the government (iv). Another hospital (ii) is planned exclusively for purposes of study or research, under the direction of the royal physicians, in which patients are to be accepted who have diseases of the kind from which the Queen might suffer. Here, too, any physician shall have the opportunity to experiment, in order that full knowledge may be gained such as may prevent the Queen, in case she should fall ill, from receiving the wrong kind of treatment.

Although in the proposals so far mentioned the destitute patients may appear to be considered too much as objects of study, in other proposals it is their welfare that receives special consideration. Proposal viii suggests that a physician and a surgeon be assigned to each hundred inhabitants of a county or a city, primarily for the benefit of sick persons among the poor; attention being drawn to the fact that the expense involved in such medical care would be made up for by the saving in the poor rates. Here, as in his earlier plans, it can be seen that Bellers did not expect much from merely altruistic motives.

The duty of the government with regard to the advancement of science and of public health appears to Bellers to be of even broader scope. He suggests (v) that a public laboratory and observation clinic be established for the preparation and testing of new remedies, and (vii) that there be official publication of the useful or harmful effects of such remedies; and he further demands (x) that there be a sort of bureau of information in the College of Surgeons, in which any physician can get advice and through which the mistakes of treatment that have been made may be posted by way of warning. (!) He also asks (ix) that physicians be sent to India and America to investigate the native remedies there; ships' doctors might also be induced to bring back such information through the promise of payment by the government for their reports. In another proposal (xi) it is suggested that the Royal Society be given a fund for the more effective execution of their efforts toward the advancement of the knowledge of nature; and finally (xii) both Houses of Parliament are urged to name a commission to receive reports with regard to the existing status of medical science, and to watch over the laws having to do with health.

All in all, Bellers's Essay amounts to nothing less than

the proposal of a complete reorganization of the care of the public health, based on the greatest practicable advancement of the science of medicine. The state and municipal corporations are called upon to bear the burden of setting up and administering all the necessary institutions. These proposals, so far in advance of the times (state oversight of the public health has not even yet been completely established in England), can be explained as the result of Bellers's special views on questions of population.[5]

For the wealth of a state, Bellers believed, depends principally upon the density of population. High numbers, however, as we saw above [6] mean for him only latent wealth: man must be made competent to do productive work, and for this reason he insists upon education as a public duty, and insists also, consistently enough, that the productive power of each individual must be maintained as long as possible through the protection and care of his health. Bellers reckons that the premature death of each laboring man is equivalent to a loss to the state of £200;[7] the wealthy he invites to make their own estimate of how their premature death should be assessed; for according to Bellers thousands even of the wealthy die each year of curable diseases. All governmental measures connected with ordinary politics, all the interests of

[5] In connection with the formulating of specific proposals, Bellers may probably have received suggestions from his friend, the physician and naturalist Sir Hans Sloane (1660-1753).

[6] See above, p. 81 (note).

[7] Bellers reckons thus: The annual net profit of a worker is worth at least £10, which, with an average period of productivity of twenty years, amounts to £200. This figure is increased in most cases by the labor of wife and children.

English trade should yield precedence therefore to the task of "obtaining all possible knowledge of the art of healing that the whole world affords."

Bellers appended to his Essay a repetition of his suggestion, made twenty years before but never adopted, that his productive communities [8] be established; but this is of secondary importance in this connection. In spite of all his zeal there was no concrete result of either proposal. Even in Quaker circles, a call which he issued in the last year of his life for the erection of a hospital was apparently unheard. In the eighteenth century no great progress was made in the science of medicine in England, any more than in most of the countries of Europe; the Quakers, however, were responsible for a few moves of considerable significance.

John Fothergill, one of the few Quaker physicians, already known to us as the founder of Ackworth School, pleaded for improved sanitary conditions in London in various respects—as, for instance, through the removal of graveyards from within the city. He also published the results of his investigations into the relation between sickness and weather conditions,[9] and attempted to secure the official registration of births, deaths, and burials. His conception of his profession is typical of the Quaker: he refused, to use his own words, to practice the art of healing as a means of earning money, with the same indignation with which he would reject a proposal to commit a crime or to live extravagantly. It often happened that he not only treated patients without charging a fee, but even

[8] See above, p. 76.
[9] His conclusions, published regularly in the *Gentleman's Magazine*, are also said to have been the first weather reports.

gave them assistance amounting to considerable sums of money.[10]

The idea that the task of easing distress and drying the tears of trouble was to be looked upon as a special privilege of physicians was emphasized later by William Allen, chemist at Guy's Hospital, London, in an address to his students.[11] He, too, was deeply interested in the advancement of medicine in England; and to him must be credited in part the establishment of a hospital for vaccination in London in 1803, the blessings of which, as his biographer writes, only his contemporaries could properly appreciate.[12] During his numerous journeys on the Continent, Allen visited not only prisons, but hospitals and other institutions for the public welfare, in order to utilize hints thus secured for the benefit of England; for at the beginning of the nineteenth century England was without doubt behind other nations in this respect.

One of the chief obstacles to organized work of this kind was, evidently, the lack of organized groups of women in the churches serving as deaconesses or as sisters of charity. Although in the Latin countries women had been made use of for various social purposes as early as the seventeenth century [13]—Francis de Sales and Vincent de Paul had created extensive organizations in the time of Louis XIV—the Protestant nations hesitated a long time to imitate these institutions because they had had a Roman Catholic origin. In Germany the nursing associations did

[10] See James H. Tuke, *A Sketch of the Life of John Fothergill,* published by the Centenary Committee, Ackworth School 1879.

[11] James Sherman, *Memoir of William Allen,* Philadelphia [1851], p. 33.

[12] Sherman, *op. cit.,* p. 28.

[13] See, for instance Gerhard Uhlhorn, *Die Christliche Liebesthätigkeit* . . . (see note 2), 2d edition Stuttgart 1893, p. 640ff.

not make their appearance until the time of the Wars of Liberation (1813-1814), and were more fully developed and organized later by Amalie Sieveking and Theodor Fliedner; and it was the Quakers who attempted to transplant the idea to England.

The new element in the German practice, which was different even from the Quaker nursing undertaken from motives of love, was the fact that nursing outside the hospitals was raised in status to be a life profession for educated women. With the help of Elizabeth Fry, who consulted personally with Fliedner, the women members of the family of Samuel Gurney, under the patronage of the Queen Dowager, set up the first organization for training of this kind [14] in 1840. A very careful selection was made of persons naturally fitted for nursing, and they were given a careful preliminary training in public hospitals, and then, after a period of trial, received as "sisters." The requirements were those which for the most part are still the usual ones: the training institution sent the sisters out on cases, in return for fees proportional to the circumstances of the patients (usually amounting to less than the actual cost), and paid them a certain amount of salary and supplied them with lodgings at times when they were not in service. During their residence in the institution, the sisters were expected to devote themselves to destitute invalids in the neighborhood.

There was no lack of opportunity for this institution to engage in much needed charitable work. Even Florence Nightingale took her helpers from here when she set out

[14] See *Memoir of the Life of Elizabeth Fry* . . . edited by two of her daughters, London and Philadelphia 1847, ii, 405.

for the Crimean War. The Association has survived to the present day [15] and has been the occasion of the starting of other institutions, similar in nature but differing from those in Germany in that the latter accepted all competent women willing to serve without regard to their social status. Uhlhorn refers to the fact that the English point of view could not be reconciled to the acceptance of all competent applicants, regardless of the question of rank, and that it thus interfered with the full development of the system of nursing in England.[16]

II. CARE OF THE INSANE

The idea that those who are mentally deranged are merely sick, and are in many cases curable, is of thoroughly modern origin.[17] In the Middle Ages they were considered on a par with criminals, and were held accountable for their behavior, or even subjected at times to capital punishment.[18] More humane was the practice of rendering them harmless by confining them in prisons or workhouses—a duty which apparently rested only upon the local charitable society, as insane persons who were not residents of the district were driven away, forcibly if necessary. Further progress was marked by the creation of institutions designed especially for the insane. This step was, however, by no means accompanied by the introduc-

[15] Institution of Nursing Sisters, 16 Broad Street Building, Bishopsgate, London.

[16] Uhlhorn, *op. cit.* (see note 13), p. 739.

[17] It was not until the time of the French Revolution that Philippe Pinel (1745-1826), the physician, ventured to remove the chains from the insane in the hospital and asylum at Bicêtre, near Paris, and to accord them medical treatment.

[18] Uhlhorn, *op. cit.,* p. 418.

tion of adequate care: the insane were treated like wild beasts, and were customarily exhibited to visitors as curiosities. Thus, in the first great English insane asylum, the Bethlem Hospital, or Bedlam, opened in London in 1676, such exhibitions were permitted until 1770, and constituted a source of some little income.[19] Conditions in St. Luke's Hospital, which was opened in London in 1715, and was also exclusively for the care of the insane, are said to have been somewhat better; but further institutions were not established for a while, so that the majority of the destitute insane were still confined in prisons and workhouses. The philanthropist John Howard, forerunner of the Quakers in the care of prisoners, reports as late as 1784 that idiots and feeble-minded were sometimes kept in penal institutions, and served as the butt of the ridicule of the idle visitors at the court proceedings. It had by that time been made a legal requirement, however, that they should be separated from other prisoners.

It can be safely assumed that the Quakers did not expose those of their members who were insane to treatment of this sort, because—if on no other evidence—they never availed themselves of public support in any form. Moreover, an epistle of the Six Weeks' Meeting from the year 1671 has been recently published, suggesting "That frends doe seeke some place convenient In or about ye Citty wherein they may put any person that may be distracted or troubled in minde, that soe they may not be put amongst ye world's people or Run about ye

[19] Daniel Hack Tuke, *Chapters in the History of the Insane . . .*, London 1882.

Streets." [20] And two years later a certain John Goodson
offered to erect a large house for "distempered and dis-
composed persons," and apparently carried his plan [21]
out. Particularly noteworthy is the fact that this Friend
was a physician; it is clear, therefore, that Quakers were
among the first to recognize the necessity of medical
treatment for the insane, and cures were no longer
thought of as being principally effected through prayer,
as might perhaps be inferred from Fox's Journal. I have
not been able to obtain further information about the history of this Quaker insane asylum; presumably it was
soon given up, for toward the end of the eighteenth century regrets are expressed at the necessity of putting
Friends who were insane under the care of those of other
denominations, as their condition was often unfavor-
ably affected by the treatment they received. [22] Moreover, the feelings of Quakers were outraged by the
almost universally rigorous treatment accorded the
insane.

The initiative for the establishment of an insane asylum
according to new principles came from William Tuke in
York. Supported by Lindley Murray and a few others,
he laid the matter before the Quarterly Meeting of
March, 1792; and a few months later there was held a

[20] Bedford Pierce, *The Treatment of the Insane*, in *Friends' Quarterly
Examiner,* vol. xxxvi (1902), p. 74, reprints this from the instructions
sent down by the Six Weeks' Meeting.

[21] Beck and Ball, p. 130.

[22] At the end of the eighteenth century there were, besides the two
above-mentioned insane asylums, wards for the insane in various public
hospitals (in London, Manchester, Liverpool, Norwich and Bristol), and
also three or four private insane asylums.

special meeting for "the purpose of taking into consideration the propriety of providing a retired habitation, with
necessary advice, attendance, etc., for Members of our
Society and others in profession with us, who may be in a
state of Lunacy or so deranged in mind (not Idiots) as to
require such a provision." [23] The details of the financial
endowment, the location and administration of the institution itself, about which agreement had been reached in
the meeting, were soon published, and contributions were
invited. The plan at first called out many objections,
partly because of the unfortunate experience which
Quakers had had with an asylum for the insane opened
in 1777, which in spite of the best of intentions had soon
fallen into a terrible condition. To dispel doubts from
this and similar causes, various meetings of this and the
next following year issued explanatory statements, which
give full information as to the fundamental principles of
the contemplated institution.

In consideration of the lower cost of real estate, and
the more rural character of the environs, York was chosen
as the location rather than London. York was preferred
to smaller places because it was the seat of a fairly large
quarterly meeting, so that, as was desirable, more or less
frequent meetings of a considerable number of contribu-
tors could be held. The money necessary for the building
and maintenance of the asylum was to come from paid-up
capital sums, in exchange for which annuities were to be
issued, paid from gifts and annual contributions. A gift

[23] Samuel Tuke, *Description of the Retreat,* London and Philadelphia
1813, p. 20.

of a specified minimum amount—the minimum being set relatively low or high according to whether the gift came from an individual or a group—conferred upon the donor the right to participate in the management and to nominate an indigent patient to be received at the lowest rate. The charge for the complete maintenance of a patient— the cost of clothing alone being excluded—was set at first at 14 or 15 shillings a week. It was expected that even well-to-do patients would be glad to secure accommodations in such an institution, "although they would have to pay well for them."

The treatment of the patients, the technique of which had to be learned by experience, will be discussed later;[24] but we may observe here that from the very beginning the patients were provided with opportunity for agricultural activity, which was engaged in not only as an aid toward making the institution self-supporting, but as a suitable employment for the patients.

In spite of the unfavorable reception of the plan in the beginning, and the very small amount of publicity given to the project—active propaganda was intentionally avoided, as only those contributions were desired which were wholly voluntary—the financial situation turned out to be unexpectedly favorable. The necessary endowment was soon considered assured. By the end of 1794 a suitable tract of land was acquired, and the building was begun. *Hoc fecit amicorum caritas in humanitatis argumentum* (The love of friends built this as an evidence of humanity) was the wording of the inscription on the foundation stone, signalizing the spirit of the place. A year and a

[24] See below, p. 157.

half later (May 1, 1796) the doors were formally opened.[25]

The institution, which at first was provided with accommodations for only thirty patients, was soon filled; even before the end of the century an enlargement was necessary. At the same time the contributions rose in even greater degree,[26] so that patients who were entirely destitute could be cared for without charge. Moreover, the charges made to paying patients remained lower than the charges which were customary in other institutions, in spite of the comparatively comfortable conditions there, and the greater cost of treatment. The complete abolition of restraint in chains—a relief which in other institutions was not accorded even to the King[27]—required a larger personnel for oversight; the medical attention was more careful than in other insane asylums, where the customary methods of cure were bleeding and starving. Great importance was attached to keeping the patients occupied and interested or amused; the burden of this task was carried chiefly by women Friends. A spirit of friendly coöperation overcame any feeling of repugnance or abhorrence toward the insane—a feeling which unfortunately dominated wide circles of people in connection

[25] Various publications of Samuel Tuke, the grandson of the founder, give accounts of the nature of the activities carried on there; for instance, the *Description,* etc., referred to above (note 23). See also *Sketch of the Origin, Progress, and Present State of the Retreat . . .,* drawn up by direction of the General Meeting, for distribution among the subscribers, York 1828.

[26] Even in 1799 the income nearly equaled the expenses. As security for the annuities, reckoned at 5% interest, all the personal and real property of the Retreat was pledged.

[27] George III, as is well known, had his first attacks of insanity in 1765, and in 1810 his condition became incurable.

with victims of far less harmful defects, as, for instance, the deaf-mutes.[28]

The percentage of cures in York Retreat is characterized as being good; but specific figures are lacking. Samuel Tuke's first essay (*Description,* etc.: see note 23), which acquainted the public with the new method, was held in high esteem, and without question did much to bring about an improvement in the care of the insane. People from various European countries and from the United States turned to York to secure further information and guidance in the reform of existing institutions and the establishment of new ones. York received many visits from interested persons; and although Tuke himself got his ideas for the successive improvements in the institution from the outside, the Retreat acquired the reputation of being a school for alienists and a model asylum.[29]

These results, attained by the Quakers, influenced the manner in which the state cared for the insane. A commission appointed by the House of Commons, which investigated insane asylums for two months during the year 1815, called the founder of the Retreat into consultation as an expert, though he was now over eighty-two

[28] In America deaf-mute girls were persecuted as if accursed, and it was a Quaker, Anthony Benezet, who first interested himself in their plight and gave them instruction.

[29] Thus Parchappe, Inspector General of the Service des Aliénés (in charge of the insane) in France, writes in 1853: "York Retreat, of which Samuel Tuke published a description in 1813, was considered to be the school at which alienists should receive their training, and the model to which they should conform. The creation and organization of this establishment has had a very great influence upon the development of good methods of treatment and upon the improvement of asylums in England." D. H. Tuke, *Chapters,* etc., . . ., p. 131, quoting from J. B. M. Parchappe, *Des Principes à suivre dans la fondation et la construction des aisles d'aliénés,* Paris 1853, p. 226.

years old. About the same time Samuel Tuke published some practical proposals, based upon his experience, for the establishment of insane asylums for the poor,[30] of which there was urgent need.[31] He demands even for these poorest among the poor that the prisonlike character of the asylums should be abandoned, for the reason that wholesome and cheerful accommodations are beneficial to the health of the patients.

He sets up the following as the most important basic principles of administration: rigid separation of the patients according to sex; classification according to degree of insanity; and constant oversight of the inmates by wardens, and effective control of the latter by their superiors. The hideous conditions in the hospitals for the poor, in which there were also some insane patients, were largely the result of lack of suitable control of the wardens.

An initial, though small, result of the labors of the Quaker pioneers came to pass with the law of 1819; though the erection of asylums was not provided for by law until 1828,[32] at which time also the overseers of the poor and the justices of the peace were required to report cases of insanity and see that the sufferers were provided for. Thorough reform ensued finally as a result of the law of 1845, the "Magna Charta of the insane," which assured a home and proper care to all, and established

[30] *Practical Hints on the Construction and Economy of Pauper Lunatic Asylums*, York 1815.

[31] As can be seen from *The Philanthropist*, i, 357ff., down to 1811 very little was attempted in the line of public care of the insane, and terrible conditions prevailed in the insane wards of the hospitals for the poor.

[32] See Sir George Nicholls, *A History of the English Poor Law*, London 1854, ii, 193, 212.

a permanent commission on insanity. Thus the people at large finally came to enjoy the advantages of which Quakers had had the benefit for fifty years. By way of preventing any relaxing of diligence, the practice was introduced in 1853 of making an annual report on insanity among the poor.

York Retreat has not lost in importance in the course of the years. Now, as formerly, it cares for the insane members of the Society of Friends and, so far as accommodations permit (the institution is now equipped to take 175 patients) takes in persons in whom members have some interest, as well as the general public; and contributions for its support come from persons outside the Quaker circle. The various meetings contribute annual sums, according to their size and the ability of their members to pay; and the board of overseers, all of whom are Quakers, give their services without pay.

In recent times the Quakers have taken up the care of the insane in connection with foreign missions. The first asylum for the insane in Palestine owes its origin to the missionary Theophilus Waldmeier, who left the Roman Catholic Church to join the Quakers.[33] He was acquainted with the terrible plight of the insane in the Holy Land,[34] and after he had studied the arrangements in York he issued an appeal in 1897 calling for the establishment of an interdenominational and international insane asylum. The plan attracted some little attention in England, where the Queen accepted the rôle of patroness,

[33] See *The Autobiography of Theophilus Waldmeier, Missionary*, London [1887].

[34] They were generally kept in dark, damp cellars and chained with heavy chains.

and also on the Continent and in America. The liberality of the contributions soon made possible the realization of the idea; and the finished asylum, built in Asfuriyeh, near Beirut, according to the pavilion plan, was opened in 1900.

The value of this institution springs not only from the expert care extended to the individual inmates (in 1905 the institution accommodated 148 patients), but also from the battle with superstition which emanated from it,[35] and the training of natives to be nurses. And so, in accordance with experience in other lands, the hospital-asylum may prove here also to be an important factor in the uplift of the common people.

[35] Up to this time the treatment of the insane had consisted mainly in efforts to exorcise demons.

CHAPTER FIVE

PRISON REFORM

In the humanitarian activities which we have hitherto considered, the Quakers concerned themselves primarily with the welfare of members of their own Society; and only as a secondary result, if at all, did the benefits of those activities extend to outsiders. Their interest in prison reform, however, arose entirely from their desire to be of benefit to non-Quakers. For the help given to their own members who languished in prison, who from the very first were maintained by the meeting, was a natural part of the general care extended to members in need. The subject that will occupy us in the present chapter is the personal work of the Quakers in behalf of prisoners in general, and their influence upon legislation and the administration of the law, undertaken with the purpose of reforming the penal code.

Not until the beginning of the nineteenth century can any effect of these labors be observed; and the work for prison reform was carried on, not as the result of any official action of the Society, but, like other types of humanitarian work, as the private concern of individual philanthropists. With regard to the fundamental ideas, they followed, perhaps unconsciously, the great Quakers who had preceded them. The Society had early emphasized the close connection between poverty, neglect of education, alcoholism, and crime, and had recognized the actual encouragement of crime resulting from the deficiencies of the law and its execution.[1] They had abundant opportunity to assemble a body of practical experience in such matters, for after the Restoration they populated the prisons literally by hundreds or often, indeed, by thousands.

And Quaker prisoners, whether they were confined because of their mere membership in the Society, or because they had created some public disturbance in the observance of their religious principles, were almost always treated like common criminals.[2] Their sense of justice did not permit them to ease the hardships of their situation by giving the customary bribes to the jailers. They refused, as a matter of principle, to pay the various charges[3] demanded often even for the most miserable sort of accommodations, and thus had to put up with the full measure of wretchedness endured by prisoners who had no money to pay. The diaries of the first traveling ministers, who were bitterly persecuted, give an idea of

[1] See Fox's *Journal*, i, 71, and his address *To the Protector and Parliament of England*, London 1658; Thomas Lawson, *Appeal to Parliament concerning the Poor, that there may not be a Beggar in England*, London 1660; Bellers's address to the Lord Mayor, in *An Essay towards the Improvement of Physick, in Twelve proposals*, London 1714, and *Essays about the Poor, Manufactures, Trade, Plantations, and Immorality*, London 1699, p. 1: "It is affecting to consider that the Bodies of many Poor, which might and should be Temples for the Holy Ghost to dwell in, are the Receptacles so much of Vice and Vermine."

[2] In *The First Publishers of Truth*, edited by Norman Penney, London 1907, p. 343ff., William Charles Braithwaite gives a collection of the laws on account of which the early Quakers were persecuted.

[3] In exceptional cases, however, jailers who had shown a kindly spirit toward Quaker prisoners were rewarded by the meeting after the prisoners had been set free. See Beck and Ball, p. 232.

what they had to endure in prison;⁴ they afford a picture, with unprintable details, of the terrible abuses which prevailed almost everywhere.

Not so much by way of easing their own lot—their faith triumphed over the bitterest physical discomfort—as from general interest in the public welfare, the Quakers demanded a thorough reform in these conditions. Just as in their efforts to improve the system of poor relief, so here it was the government which, in their view, was to be appealed to for help; individual efforts, obviously doomed to failure in those unstable times, were apparently not even seriously considered.

Repeatedly, by memorials to Parliament and to various officials, the Quakers drew attention to the necessity for reform—to the obligation that rested upon the state to extend its care even to those among its subjects who had broken its laws.⁵ Along with certain strange ideas springing from their desire that the ancient Mosaic code might be restored—for they looked upon this as a complete panacea—even the earliest documents contain a number of very practical suggestions. In order to be able to appraise them intelligently, we must glance quickly at the conditions existing at that time.

The prisons were almost uniformly dungeonlike or underground rooms which, as they were mostly overcrowded

⁴ The jailers often interfered with or altogether prevented the visits of the women who brought food to their fellow members, and often even encouraged the other prisoners to take away from the Quakers such food as they did receive.

⁵ See Fox's address *To the Protector*, etc., (1658), and *To the Parliament of the Commonwealth of England*, London 1659; also *An Instruction to Judges and Lawyers, that they may act and Judge as did the Judges of old*, etc., London [1660].

and never properly ventilated, were crusty with filth and alive with vermin. Those who were diseased in body or mind were not separated from the others; there were even complaints that the jailers neglected to remove the bodies of those who had died. The prisoners had to provide their own food and clothing, and as a result many had to endure hunger and cold, and all were dependent upon the humor of the jailers. The low grade of these officials constituted one of the chief evils. They received no regular pay, but made their money from trafficking in the food and drink for the prisoners and from the above-mentioned fees, which were set at any figure their self-interest suggested. In other respects also they were not subject to any adequate supervision or control: the management of a prison was not considered a fit occupation for a decent person.

From these causes alone it is easy to see that a term of imprisonment must have had a demoralizing effect; but the situation was aggravated by the fact that accused prisoners awaiting trial were herded together with convicted criminals of all ages and stages; even the sexes were not always separately housed. The prisons were thus breeding-places of crime—the more so since with few exceptions there was no sort of occupation to divert the attention of the inmates even for short intervals, and to offset the effects of mutual demoralization.

In view of these conditions, which occasioned very little concern or were considered at most as necessary evils, the Quakers contributed a new conception to penology: *imprisonment should not be viewed as a punishment, but as a means to reform.* Hence they protested against chains, confinement of the prisoners in narrow cages, and other such cruelties. Strictness, but not barbarous tyranny, should, in their opinion, characterize the treatment accorded prisoners; and the jailers should be reliable persons. Accommodations good enough to be above reproach from the standpoint of health should be given to all, without special fee; and the jailers should be forbidden to sell alcohol to their charges. It cannot be definitely proved that the first Quakers urged the need of classification; but it is entirely in accord with their other suggestions, and was perhaps taken for granted as self-evident. Again and again, on the other hand, they emphasized the need of occupation for all prisoners, as a means both for their moral rehabilitation and for the support of their dependents.

While ineffectual efforts were being made to bring about these desirable changes, the way was being paved for a few reforms of the law even in the time of the Protectorate. It seemed more important for the time being to change the penal code so as to lessen the number of prisoners than to improve the treatment of those actually convicted. The most serious matter was the lack of proper proportion between the punishment and the gravity of the offense, against which protests had been made again and again since the Civil Wars.[6] The existing law, which imposed the death penalty for 150 different crimes, which struck down the thief who had filched only a small sum as well as the murderer, inevitably destroyed all sense of justice in the popular mind. Cromwell himself appre-

[6] For instance, in Lilburne's petition, as early as 1647. See S. R. Gardiner, *History of the Great Civil War*, London 1886, iii, 72.

ciated that such conditions were indefensible. He is said
to have expressed the opinion, on one occasion, that the
law was of use only to the lawyers, and merely served for
the oppression of the poor by the rich.[7] In spite of the
inevitable opposition, Parliament appointed a commission
in 1652 to consider the weaknesses of the law as it stood
and to suggest the quickest and best remedies. The abolition of the death penalty except for murder, which Fox
had vehemently urged,[8] was effected in 1653 through the
pardon of all criminals convicted of other crimes; and in
addition certain relief was afforded to debtors. Steps
were taken also for the abolition of the Court of Chancery, which was notorious for dragging out the cases that
came before it and for partisanship in its decisions. The
unified regulation of the courts was not put through under
Cromwell, however, and with the Restoration the reaction set in at once. All existing reform laws were repealed, and those which had been planned but not carried
out were dropped.[9]

If the Puritans had remained in power longer, the
plight of the prisoners would have also been improved,
and individual activity would doubtless have followed
the state's lead. The early Christians, whom the Quakers
strove so zealously to imitate, had concerned themselves
with the spiritual and bodily welfare of captives and pris-

[7] Charles Firth, *Oliver Cromwell and the Rule of the Puritans in England,* London and New York 1900, pp. 304-305.

[8] Fox proposed, for instance, that thieves should be obligated to the
restoration of some multiple of the amount they had stolen, but should
not be punished in any other way.

[9] There was evidently more of a protest against Puritanism in this
step than against the irregularity of Cromwell's régime. Edicts which
were to the advantage of agriculture, as for instance the Navigation
Acts, were at once confirmed by Charles II.

oners; and this custom, though it lapsed and was forgotten during the Middle Ages, had been reintroduced on the Continent by edicts of the Protestant Church. In England, however, the extension of such evangelical principles, even gradually, to other matters was completely prevented for the time being by the return of the Stuarts. The persecution of the Puritan faith was bound to have the effect of putting a premium upon brutality and frivolity. Instead of regarding the convicts as their fellow men, in need of help, most people looked upon them and the spectacle of their sufferings as a source of amusement. Thus Macaulay relates how certain distinguished lords arranged pleasure jaunts to Bridewell on court days, in order to see the women flogged there. Executions and the preceding religious service, at which the worshipers could enjoy the terror of the victims, were a favorite entertainment even into the nineteenth century.

But in spite of the fact that such proofs of moral degradation gave the characteristic stamp to the régime of the last Stuarts, there was never a time when protests were not raised and private attempts made to effect reform. Following Fox and Penn, who had never allowed themselves to be deterred from publishing their ideas by the prevalence of anti-Puritan tendencies, the Quaker John Bellers came forward toward the end of the seventeenth century as a typical representative of the Society—laboring, to be sure, more in behalf of their social message than their theology. Various of his far-seeing plans for the amelioration of social ills have been outlined in the preceding pages.

PRISON REFORM

The actual care of prisoners is a matter of secondary concern for Bellers; he lays primary emphasis upon preventive treatment of those classes of society which are especially predisposed to criminality. First and foremost he is concerned for the homeless orphans, the so-called "Black Guard," who, swarming through the streets of London without training or oversight, fell a prey to every evil influence. He points out the duty of society with regard to them; for, however repulsive they may appear, they are after all the children of the community.[10] They ought to be properly trained, so that their souls may not be needlessly lost to the world hereafter, "nor useful men"—here again the practical-minded Quaker betrays himself—"lost to this present world." [11]

The duty of society to do what could be done to further the latent possibilities of development in any man, even the sodden criminal, appeared to Bellers to be self-evident; and in accord with this view he was necessarily opposed to capital punishment.[12] His predecessor Fox, who in this case attributed everlasting validity to the precepts of the Bible, had acknowledged the death penalty as a just atonement for the crime of murder; but Bellers, taking a more advanced stand, initiates the propaganda of the

[10] See his address to the Lord Mayor and other persons in public positions, in *An Essay towards the Improvement of Physick,* etc., London 1714. These homeless waifs were probably for the most part illegitimate children who had been deserted by their parents, and kept themselves from starving by begging and stealing. "Many of them may have descended from eminent citizens," says Bellers.

[11] In *An Epistle to Friends of the Yearly, Quarterly, and Monthly Meetings,* dated March 12, 1724, Bellers again stresses the obligation of the community to care for these children.

[12] See *Some Reasons against Putting of Felons to Death,* in *Essays about the Poor,* etc. (see note 1), p. 17ff.

Quakers for utter abolition of the death penalty.[18] In his view, society does enough for its own protection if the criminal is made harmless by strict confinement; execution constitutes a "blot upon religion" (a reminiscence of the fifth petition of the Lord's Prayer: "Forgive us our trespasses, as we forgive those who trespass against us"). For the responsibility for a criminal act cannot be laid exclusively upon the criminal: the crime is partly caused by unfortunate environment and bad training. Accordingly a treatment aiming at reform should be undertaken even in prison, especially by accustoming the prisoners to productive work. In the course of time this could be followed up by marriage (!) or by deportation to a colony. Bellers is optimist enough to think that permanent reform can be attained by such measures for the great majority of criminals.

Even in these detailed positions the typically Quaker attitude remained something strange and unintelligible to most persons. The conception of the criminal as at least partially a victim of conditions created by society, and the deduction that he therefore had certain claims upon this same society, and that society was under moral obligation to do what it could toward his reform, required a type of social thinking to which the England of that time had by no means attained. But the great humanitarian exhibited an unwearied zeal in promoting his plans. After many addresses to Parliament and to executive departments, which had no discernible effect, he tried, as late as

[18] It thus appears that credit for priority in agitating the abolition of capital punishment, which is usually given to the Italian jurist Cesare Bonesano de Beccaria (1738-1794) because of his essay *Dei delitti e delle pene* (On crimes and punishments), 1764, belongs in reality to Bellers.

the year before his death, to arouse sympathy for the prisoners at least within the membership of the Society of Friends. In an epistle addressed to the whole member-ship,[14] he expresses the hope that many Friends may feel moved to interest themselves in the miserable inmates of the prisons. In order to convince the prisoners them-selves of the good intentions of those who would help them, he considers it desirable that there should be some large-scale proof of unselfish interest, such as an annual banquet for all prisoners in need of food. As a result of interest gained through the enjoyment of material things, it might be possible, as the example of the Gospel shows, to win them for something higher.

But Bellers goes beyond this, in accord with the usual practice of the Quakers, in laying a firm economic founda-tion before attempting any upbuilding of the spirit. Like Fox, he believes that work should be provided for the prisoners, appropriate to their abilities and to life in jail, which, besides providing the means for eking out their subsistence during their imprisonment in any way that might be necessary, would serve to awaken a permanent urge to industry. Not until very late is there any recom-mendation that practical suggestions for getting along in the world should be combined with moral maxims, which were to be brought to the attention of the prisoners in the form of placards, and further disseminated in tracts.

No records have been found reporting the result of this challenge; but we may in all probability safely assume that there was no report to make. It is true that during the first decades of its existence the Society had felt a

[14] See note 11.

lively concern for the moral uplift of certain groups which appeared to be a menace to public order. Their services in disciplining bands of robbers in northern England had been noted with approval even by the officials; but at the time of Bellers's Epistle (1724), the internal affairs of the Society absorbed all their available energies. The first half of the eighteenth century was a period of outer retrogression, of inner stagnation, of the Quaker movement, and this situation is a sufficient explanation of the fact that the matter of caring for prisoners long remained a mere pious aspiration.

This statement, however, is true only for England; in Pennsylvania, on the other hand, the Quaker ideal found early recognition. The "Laws agreed upon in England," appended to the Frame of Government of 1682, contain the provision (article x): "All prisons shall be workhouses for felons, vagrants, and loose and idle persons, rakes, and loafers"; [15] and "All prisons shall be free, as to fees, food, and lodging" (article xiii). This attempt of Penn to make prisons into reformatories, and to maintain them at public expense, was considered in those days to be as new and as striking as the religious toleration which was granted to all sects without discrimination.

There is no lack of evidence as to the way in which these measures were carried out. Thus, in the biography of Thomas Shillitoe, who labored for the welfare of prisoners in England and other countries, we read that the Philadelphia State Prison for Pennsylvania was a veri-

---

[15] See *Minutes of the Provincial Council of Pennsylvania*, Philadelphia 1852, i, 38. Imprisonment for debt did not exist in Pennsylvania until 1700.

table model.[16] In this institution the three basic elements
of good prison administration were united: compulsory
work, appropriate classification of inmates, and religious
instruction. Fiske also writes, in his work on the Quaker
colonies,[17] that Pennsylvania had distinguished itself by
the good administration of its prisons and the humanity
of their discipline, and that travelers from Europe had
acknowledged the penal institutions to be found there as
the best in the world.

Much credit is due for the attainment of such results;
but it must not be forgotten that conditions in Pennsylvania and England were not altogether comparable as
regards their adaptability to social experimenting. The
settlers in the Quaker colony constituted, so to speak, a
select group, and they had a greater degree of homogene-
ity than could be found in an ordinary cross section of a
population in which the separate individuals exhibit the
most striking contrasts because of differences of origin,
education, and wealth. It should further be noted that
the Quakers of Pennsylvania, at least in the earlier days
of the colony, enjoyed complete freedom of action in respect to their attempts to heal and to prevent social ills.
Compulsory attendance at school and the restriction of
the sale of alcohol undoubtedly had a favorable effect
upon morality. Conditions in England were fundamentally different. The interest of the state in the moral uplift
of the people amounted to almost nothing. Those who
belonged to religious groups which did appear to be inter-

[16] William Tallack, *Thomas Shillitoe, the Quaker Missionary and
Temperance Pioneer*, London 1867, p. 140.
[17] John Fiske, *The Dutch and Quaker Colonies in America*, Boston and
New York 1899, ii, 327.

ested in the introduction of a really effective social policy were disqualified for participation in the political administration by their religion.

Opportunity for individual activity was limited. What Bellers asked of Quakers in this respect exceeded perhaps the bounds of possibility; it presupposed the coöperation or at least the toleration of the authorities. The lack of this necessary condition of success explains the reluctance of the Quakers to bestir themselves even at the period when the above-mentioned distractions within the Society itself no longer existed. Only a thorough comprehension of the evils of the situation, such as would result from the interest of wide circles of people, was sufficient to create such a pressure of public opinion as would bring the efforts toward reform to fruition. The work of creating this interest—performed by others than Quakers—falls within the period between the first proposals made by the early Friends regarding the proper care of prisoners and the revival of this concern by members of the Society during the nineteenth century.

It is often said that John Howard was the first student of English prisons to present a systematic account of the conditions to be found there; but even he had his predecessors. Toward the end of the seventeenth century, the Society for Promoting Christian Knowledge began to voice protests at the conditions in the jails,[18] and in the first decades of the eighteenth century there were extensive official inspections. The cause of these inspections was a succession of appeals and complaints from prisoners, who suffered more from the high-handedness of the

[18] Georgina King Lewis, *Elizabeth Fry*, London 1910, p. 44ff.

jailers than from the restrictions imposed by law.[19] But although the reports of the commissions appointed to investigate confirmed the complaints of abuses, no steps were undertaken to remedy them.

The first attempts at actual reform in this domain are to be attributed to John Howard. Born in 1726 of a well-to-do merchant family, highly educated and informed by an active interest in social problems, this philanthropist and reformer, through his appointment as High Sheriff of Bedford, was given the oversight of the county prisons, and thus acquired the opportunity to do effective work.[20] His efforts were directed primarily toward assuring the jailers and other prison officials a fixed salary, so that the exaction of fees from the prisoners could be abolished;[21] and he strove also, by improving the sanitary conditions of the prisons, to transform them into fit habitations for human beings. On the occasion of his presence in the House of Commons, which had summoned him (in 1774) to testify regarding conditions in prisons, he submitted his proposals for reform. A law was passed in 1774, the intent of which was to embody these proposals; but, like earlier acts of Parliament, it seems to have had little effect by reason of the failure of strict enforcement.[22]

Howard engaged in personal labor with unwearied

[19] Reports on the petitions of the prisoners are to be found in J. Eliot Hodgkin, MS 15, *Report of the Historical MSS Commission*, pp. 338, 341ff.

[20] See William H. Render, *Through Prison Bars . . .*, London [1894].

[21] It was quite possible for persons who were under arrest pending trial to be acquitted, but to be unable to get out of prison because of their inability to pay the fees.

[22] This may be inferred from reports on English prisons made by Sir Thomas Fowell Buxton in 1818.

zeal, inspecting prisons within and without his county, and in many cases was able to bring about some amelioration of the condition of the prisoners. The results of his investigation of English and numerous foreign penal institutions, published in 1777,[23] may be considered to be Howard's most significant work on prison reform, and brought him honorable recognition as the author; but a thorough overhauling of the system was reserved for a later time.

Howard called himself "the plodder who goes about to collect materials for men of genius to make use of." These "men of genius" were found among the Quakers. And not by accident. It is well known that Howard had worked with Quakers. John Fothergill, for instance, had coöperated with Howard in his work in the prisons with word and deed. It was he also who, with the assistance of a few fellow Quakers from all over England, had collected a fund for the amelioration of the wretchedness of the French prisoners of war; and Quakers had contributed more than a quarter of the entire sum raised. These labors were directed, to be sure, at only one aspect of the whole problem of prison reform, and not the most important one at that—for the chief aim of the reformers was to raise convicted criminals out of the atmosphere of crime; yet they served as the occasion of renewed interest in the plight of the prisoners.

We have already referred to Thomas Shillitoe, who devoted himself to the spiritual and bodily needs of prison

[23] John Howard, *The State of the Prisons in England and Wales, with Preliminary Observations and an Account of some Foreign Prisons,* 4th edition London 1792.

inmates. The permanent results of Shillitoe's activity appear to have been very slight, probably owing to the fact that he, like other Quakers, made no effort to train a group of helpers. The efforts of individual workers, no matter how zealous their philanthropy, seemed of little avail in the face of the magnitude of the evil to be overcome. The organization necessary to effect any lasting prison reform did not come into existence until more than a quarter of a century after Howard's death.

Such organization was brought about by the efforts of Elizabeth Fry.[24] This remarkable woman was first stirred to an interest in prisons by an American Quaker, Stephen Grellet. In the course of a visit to England in 1813, Grellet visited a number of penal institutions [25] with William Forster, and, shocked by the fearful conditions in the women's section of the Newgate prison, he appealed for help to Elizabeth Fry, who already had given evidence of her lively sympathy for the poor and needy in distress. Unhesitatingly she added this labor of love to her other charitable activities, and her efforts were crowned with unexpected success. Having heard from Stephen Grellet that most of the children who were in prison with their mothers—many of them had been born there—were entirely naked, she made the distribution of clothing her first point of contact with the convicts. Her impressions

[24] The conversion of Elizabeth Fry (then Gurney) by the American preacher William Savery constitutes a story of touching interest. See Francis R. Taylor, *Life of William Savery*, New York 1925, p. 428ff.
[25] See *Memoirs of the Life and Gospel Labours of Stephen Grellet*, edited by Benjamin Seebohm, 2 vols., London 1860, i, 220-226.

THE QUAKERS AS PIONEERS

of this first visit have been repeatedly described by herself and her biographer.[26]

The enormous increase in crime during the preceding years (the number of convicts in the jails doubled between 1810 and 1817) had brought about an unendurable over-crowding of the prisons. Newgate, designed for 500, housed 822 in 1813.[27] The situation was exactly parallel to that which the first Quakers had cried out against more than a century and a half earlier. Young and old, criminals, insane, and debtors, were all locked up together; visitors were admitted or excluded according to the whim of the jailers. The money which the prisoners were accustomed to beg from them was at once transmuted into liquor; for there were no regulations governing its sale or use. Neither beds nor other furniture, not even the common necessities, were provided; the 300 women with their numerous children, whom Elizabeth Fry found in entirely inadequate quarters, were obliged to sleep, wash, cook, and eat on the floor. They were entirely in the power of two wardens. No occupation was provided for those who were well; nor was any care given to the sick, who lay around helpless on the ground.

Mrs. Fry and the few Quaker women whom she induced to help her did not attempt at first to do more than mitigate the worst cases of physical need and, occasionally, say a few words of religious admonition. The claims of her own family kept Elizabeth Fry herself away from

[26] See Render, *op. cit.;* Georgina King Lewis, *op. cit.,* p. 47. See also *Memoir of the Life of Elizabeth Fry with Extracts from her Journal and Letters,* edited by two of her daughters, 2 vols., Philadelphia 1847, i, 225; Laura E. Richards, *Elizabeth Fry, the Angel of the Prisons,* New York and London 1916, p. 100.

[27] E. Hooper, *Newgate,* in *Daily Chronicle,* November 11, 1909.

London over a period of several years; not until 1816 was she able to take up her work for prison reform on any very great scale. Various forces united at that time to further her efforts.

In 1815 her brother-in-law, Thomas Fowell Buxton, had founded the Society for the Improvement of Prison Discipline; at the same time a delegation of the London prison administration had been entrusted with the inspection of various prisons, and had instituted various minor changes even in Newgate. These changes, however, extended only to such matters as the provision of more space, and the shutting off of the prisoners from visitors by means of gratings or screens; nothing was undertaken for the improvement of conditions from the moral standpoint. Afterwards, as before, the women passed their time at card playing and vulgar quarreling; in so far as they could read at all, they amused themselves with the veriest trash. Yet even these creatures, low though they had fallen, were not wholly without a sense of what they needed: they complained continually over their enforced idleness.

In view of the impossibility of procuring work at once for these women prisoners—such a project could only be carried out through the formation of a fairly large auxiliary committee—a beginning was made by instructing them in the care of their children. They were encouraged to choose a teacher from among their number, whose work in giving the children elementary instruction was overseen and assisted by the visiting women.[28]

The next step, undertaken (in 1817) in an effort to

[28] See *Memoir of the Life of Elizabeth Fry* . . ., i, 282ff.

provide all adults with employment, was the foundation in Newgate of the Association for the Improvement of Women Prisoners, composed at first of a clergyman and his wife and eleven members of the Society of Friends. In spite of the skepticism of the officials, a meeting of all the prisoners was held, at which the plans were explained. Elizabeth Fry pointed out that the Association had no disciplinary authority and did not want to exercise any compulsion; their only wish was to help the prisoners. They were to subject themselves only to such regulations as they themselves might approve, and provide for the maintenance of order through their own appointees.

The proposal met with ready acceptance. A division into groups was undertaken, each under the direction of one of the inmates; though owing to the limitations of space it was impossible to give each group separate accommodations. A few members of the Association remained in the prison during the entire day, to provide general oversight; and in addition the Association employed a matron from their own funds, who lived in the prison.

After these preparations the Association could seriously attack the task of providing the prisoners with work; and they were effectively assisted by the coöperation of a few London firms. It was found possible to organize, within the prison, a regular manufactory for making various kinds of clothing. Whenever large-scale purchasers failed, the products of the prisoners' labor were disposed of in special sales conducted by the Association.

The thought will naturally occur to the critical reader that free laborers would be injured by the competition of the prisoners; and this consideration also received attention from Elizabeth Fry. She came to the conclusion, however, that any possible injury to the total body of the laboring class brought about by convict labor could only be of very small moment, in view of the relatively insignificant number of the convicts engaged in such labor, and that this injury, if indeed any could be proved, would be more than compensated for by the advantage to society of having the convicts employed.

In later days—Quakers stress again and again the necessity for compelling convicts to submit to employment of some kind—the so-called sloyd system was recommended, in order that this danger might be entirely eliminated. The purpose of this system was to instruct prisoners in the use of tools, and gradually to train them to a certain degree of facility.[29] The convicts, of course, could not at once develop the skill requisite to the production of salable articles; but it was easier to put up with a measure of delay when there was some guarantee that at least the necessities of life could be paid for independently of the convicts' private means.

For the initial stages, in any event, the procedure of the Association turned out to be effective. After the organization had carried on its work for a time, the Corporation of London convinced themselves of its effectiveness by a visit to Newgate. What they found surpassed their most extravagant expectations. What had hitherto been a "hell on earth" had now become a place of industrious work; the rabble of savage and unruly inmates, to

[29] William Tallack, *Penological and Preventive Principles, with Special Reference to Europe and America,* 2d edition London 1896, p. 274, refers to A. Salomon, *Teacher's Handbook of Slöjd* (sloyd), London 1891.

whom hitherto visitors durst not approach too near, had changed into a peaceable family group. At once efforts were made to render these astonishing improvements as permanent as possible. Mrs. Fry's rules, which had hitherto possessed no binding force, were incorporated into the official prison regulations; the visiting women from the Association were given the right to administer punishment; and grants of money were made to meet the expenses of the plan.

The efforts of the Association were not limited to Newgate. Gradually the range of its activities expanded so as to include more and more penal institutions, first in London, and later in many other cities of Great Britain and Ireland; though it was a number of years before its founder could write in her journal: "I believe that every jail is now being visited (1836)." Knowledge of her results had become public long before this; many came to see the miracle, and the one who was responsible for it became famous.[30] Yet Mrs. Fry, herself surprised at her success, felt only astonishment at having been the humble cause of so great a work.[31]

Not only did the women's associations steadily increase in number; the scope of their activities became more and more inclusive. Following the care of the convicts in

---

[30] Elizabeth Braithwaite Emmott, *The Story of Quakerism*. London 1908, p. 208, quotes from the *Chronicles of Newgate*: "What Mrs. Fry quickly accomplished against tremendous difficulties is one of the brightest facts in the history of philanthropy."

[31] In 1824 Elizabeth Fry writes in her journal (*Memoir*, i, 492): "It is surprising even to myself, to find what has been accomplished! How many prisons are now visited by ladies and how much is done for the inhabitants of the prison house! and what a way is made for their return from evil. It is marvellous in my eyes, that a poor instrument should have been the apparent cause of setting forward such a work."

prison there came, as a natural corollary, the care of discharged convicts, and of persons who had suffered injury
while in prison. Houses of refuge were established, the
first of which, Toothill Fields Asylum in Westminster,
was opened in 1822 by a certain Miss Neave. The prisoners who appeared most amenable to reform received
preference; and in general an attempt was made to pay
most particular attention to the worthiest, with the idea
that such a policy would serve as an incentive to industry
and good conduct.

The term of imprisonment was often followed by deportation,[32] under conditions which were particularly
likely to undo all the good which might have been labori-
ously done. Violent and demoralizing scenes were common occurrences while the prisoners were being forcibly
loaded on board ship; and during the passage sanitary
conditions were anything but favorable, and no sort of
oversight or occupation was provided. When the transported convicts arrived at their destination nobody paid
any attention to their further fate. Wholly destitute and
unfamiliar with local conditions, they were exposed to a
great variety of dangers.

As far as the women in the prison reform associations
could help in these matters, they did so. They began by
making official inquiry as to living conditions about the
ports of destination, in order to be able to prepare in
advance, as much as possible, the convicts who were to be
transported there. Raw materials were supplied to the
convicts such as they could manufacture during the voyage

[32] There was a conspicuous lack of women in the population of New
South Wales, Australia, at this time, and women convicts in particular
were often sent there to supply this lack.

into products which would be immediately salable upon their arrival. Thus an attempt was made to prevent their demoralization during the long voyage, and to render existence safer for them during their first few weeks in the strange country.[33]

For the protection of women convicts who were to be transported, the Association succeeded, after many petitions to the government, in securing the appointment of matrons to accompany them on the voyage. They also directed their efforts toward securing a less conspicuous departure. To spare the feelings of the prisoners, they were taken to the port in closed wagons, and put on board ship in relatively secluded places. And last, and perhaps not least, the visiting women evidenced their interest and good will to the convicts to the very last: they went on board the ships with them, to give them such consolation and friendly advice as they could. Elizabeth Fry herself, from 1818 to her death in 1845, visited every one, with few exceptions, of the two to five transport ships departing each year from the Thames, each containing from 200 to 500 convicts.

Just as in the matter of after care, so in preventive measures the women's associations could make only a modest beginning, and point the way to other philanthropists. Their interest turned to the numerous homeless girls in London, who, though they had often already

[33] Elizabeth Fry herself remarks in her *Observations on the Visiting, Superintendence, and Government of Female Prisoners,* London 1827, p. 64: "It generally happens that such of the female transports as obtain, from the surgeon of the vessel, a certificate of their orderly behaviour while under his care, are, on their arrival at their place of destination, immediately hired as servants by the most respectable families in the colony."

developed into practiced criminals, were still too young to be taken into a house of correction. For these a School of Discipline was opened in Chelsea. Elizabeth Fry was very anxious to have this institution taken over by the municipality; but upon the advice of Sir Robert Peel, who considered maintenance by private subscription to be incomparably more effective, the authorities refused to take the step.

Elizabeth Fry was continually active in establishing further institutions of the same sort; for the lack of educational facilities of any kind for the lower classes proved to be particularly effective in spreading criminality among children. To be sure, this great evil had already called forth the active interest of Quakers outside the women's associations. We may refer, for instance, to an organization which is associated with the names of Peter Bedford and William Allen,[34] the Society for Lessening the Causes of Juvenile Delinquency in the Metropolis. The purposes of this society were, on the one hand, to study the causes of the increase in juvenile crime in London, and on the other, to attempt to offset the harmful influences to which children were exposed, and to help and support children who had been released from jail, so as to bring them back to a decent way of life.

On account of this last point, the Society came to be called by the name "Friends of Thieves."[35] Its members were scattered over all parts of the city and visited all the various prisons; in the interest of thorough work each

[34] See William Tallack, *Peter Bedford, the Spitalfields Philanthropist*, London 1865, and James Sherman, *Memoir of William Allen*, Philadelphia [1851], p. 132.
[35] Tallack, *op. cit.*, p. 52.

member was assigned only a limited field of activity. Their investigations brought to light some tragic facts. Thousands of children lived exclusively from theft. Hunger, miserable lodgings, lack of occupation and of any sort of training inevitably suggested a life of crime to them, and confinement in the prisons generally completed their moral ruin.

The unwearied labors of the Society, and the real interest which the authorities showed in their efforts, brought about a few results; but this line of Quaker activity makes, on the whole, a less conspicuous showing than the work of Elizabeth Fry. Her personality stood out above those of the loyal women who worked with her—as, for instance, Anna Buxton and Elizabeth Pryor—and also of her male coadjutors, though these her associates deserve a certain share of the glory. A few men—Allen, Bedford, Grellet, the two Gurneys (Elizabeth Fry's brothers), and T. F. Buxton (her brother-in-law)—were among the better known men who had taken an active part in visiting the prisons; Buxton and the Gurneys undertook extensive tours of inspection and published the results of their observations. Their writings, and those of Elizabeth Fry,[36] when taken as a whole, give a conception of the gradually clarifying theory of the Quakers regarding prison reform, and the closely related matter of the reform of criminal law. Though many details of this theory

[36] Thomas Fowell Buxton, *An Enquiry whether Crime and Misery are produced or prevented by our present System of Prison Discipline;* and *Proceedings of the Ladies' Committee at Newgate in 1813,* London 1818. See also Elizabeth Fry, *Observations,* etc. (see note 33); Joseph John Gurney, *Notes on a Visit made to some of the Prisons in Scotland and the North of England, with some general observations on the subject of Prison Discipline,* London 1819.

are already familiar as a result of our consideration of practical deeds of the Quakers, we may venture to review here the outstanding points.

The demands of the Quakers are based upon two presumptions: first, that *even the convicted criminal has certain rights;* and second, that the chief purpose of imprisonment—that is, the purpose which is of greatest importance to society—is *the reform of the convict.* Let us first consider the rights of the criminal.

As a human being, with human sensibilities, the convict has a right to expect a wholesome place to live in, decent clothing and bedding, and sufficient food to sustain him. "Has a case ever been heard of in which a criminal has been sentenced to rheumatism or typhus?" asks Buxton. And he draws attention to the serious injury to health which frequently resulted from imprisonment; one who got into jail because of some trifling offense ran the risk of paying for his error with lifelong illness. According to Buxton's firm conviction, there was actually less physical suffering in the numerous hospitals which he visited than in most of the prisons.[37]

Further, the convict has a right to be protected against injury not only to his health, but to his moral life as well, although life in intimate companionship with the sort of people who constituted the prison population was almost bound to bring about moral decay. For self-preservation itself often made it necessary to adopt the methods of the other inmates. As a remedy for this evil, the Quakers demanded the separation of convicts into classes; but this

[37] As early as 1665 the Quakers had pointed out, in connection with the plague, that the epidemic claimed an especially large number of victims in the penal institutions.

policy should not lead, except in extreme cases, to solitary confinement,[38] "for man was created a social being." Forbidding the prisoners to converse, and darkening their cells, are also to be rejected, in their view, as harmful, and chains are to be given up for the same reason, as such measures for the most part have no good effects.

The recognition of these rights as evidenced by humane considerateness in the treatment of prisoners, was the prerequisite for the second point—the insistence that the reform or improvement of the prisoners should be the purpose of confinement, for their own welfare and that of society. This matter of reform, if we may stress it again, is always the primary consideration. The notion of punishment, if it appears at all, is given secondary importance. Again and again the fundamental principle is enunciated: *Prisons should be educational institutions in the true sense of the word.*

In the ideal prison, then, every factor was to be eliminated which was not in accord with this conception, such as free association of all classes of prisoners with each other, intermingling of the sexes,[39] intercourse with rela-

[38] The welfare of the other prisoners is the only consideration involved in determining when solitary confinement is justified. See *Memoir of Elizabeth Fry,* ii, 409. The English Quakers apparently offer a sharp contrast in this respect to the American Quakers; for there were many Quakers in the Association which founded the Eastern Penitentiary in Pennsylvania in 1821, in which the principle of solitary confinement was strictly adhered to. See Richard Vaux, *Brief Sketch of the Origin and History of the State Penitentiary for the Eastern District of Pennsylvania,* Philadelphia 1872, pp. 6, 14, 20ff.

[39] Buxton found that male and female prisoners were sometimes separated by being at opposite ends of a single room, with not even a lattice between; and that the jailers, in return for a gratuity, permitted free intercourse. "If invention had been racked to find out methods of corrupting female virtue, nothing more ingenious could have been discovered than the practices of the borough compter" [*i.e.,* jail].

tives and friends or with passers-by on the street, the bringing in of food, and especially of spirituous liquors, from the outside,[40] harmful diversions, etc. The elements, on the other hand, that tended to favor the reform of the prisoners were expressly specified. Three points are urged in this connection: strict discipline, work,[41] and training.

Of these, the first two are closely related. It is true that the prisoner has a natural right to human treatment; but on the other hand he must be made to feel, through strict discipline, that his crime has brought him into disgrace. Wise discipline can also effect a grading of the punishment, and at the same time inculcate useful habits of work by the assignment of labor which shall be in greater or less degree remunerative or pleasant. Work at the treadmill—the usual "hard labor"—is not considered desirable by the Quakers; at most it should be used as punishment only for a short time, especially in the case of women.

Discipline and work lead themselves easily to instruction or training. Even when prisoners are forced to labor, there should be some consideration of what will be useful to them after their discharge; and men should therefore be instructed in a trade, women in household work and sewing. Elementary school instruction should go hand in hand with the development of manual skill. In view of

[40] The fact that the procuring of the means of subsistence was left to a great extent to the prisoner himself meant that the few well-to-do prisoners could considerably lessen the severity of their sentence.

[41] Buxton says: "As idleness is one great cause of sin, industry is one great means of reformation." Even the prisoner held awaiting trial should work like the others; for, though he could not be compelled to do so, he could usually be persuaded to.

the prevalence of illiteracy,[42] it was natural for the Quakers to urge the introduction of the Lancaster system into the prisons. They considered this necessary not only for the intellectual uplift of the inmates, but also as a means of religious training, through individual study of the Bible, which they looked upon as a prerequisite to a moral and useful life.

There are also many suggestions in Quaker writings with regard to the organization of the reform work by coördinating the efforts of the officials and of volunteer workers. For the former, especially for the prison matrons, who are now demanded for all prisons, the rule is laid down: "[The matron] ought never to be chosen because the situation is suited to her wants, but only because she is suited to fill the situation" (E. Fry, in her *Observations*, p. 28). Careful selection is urgently needed. Better birth or breeding in the jailers, who are continually associated with the prisoners, appears desirable only so far as it serves to assure their respect (*Observations*, p. 29).

In addition to these reforms, it was considered important that the educated classes should have some direct means of contact with the prisoners, as by means of chaplains [43] and friendly visitors. In view of the brilliant results attained by the women, similar associations of men were urged.[44] Unselfish kindness exercises an especially

[42] It was ascertained in an investigation in 1821 that of each 100 convicts only 5 had attended national schools and 8 had attended Sunday Schools, so that 87% were entirely illiterate.

[43] The first bill for the appointment of chaplains was passed in 1814.

[44] J. J. Gurney, in his *Notes*, etc. (see note 36), devotes a whole chapter to the visiting committees. "Those who feel a real concern for the present and eternal welfare of their fellow creatures, ought to be induced

good influence upon prisoners; and visitors are also often able to give advice as to the classification of prisoners, the sort of work appropriate to them, etc., and are not open to the suspicion of being subject to political pull or of being under the influence of the clergy. The Quakers hope, if these reforms are carried out and the already existing regulations are strictly enforced, that more and more those who have hitherto been counted as lost to the community may be made into useful members of the human family.

It remains for us to consider briefly the efforts of the Quakers directed toward legal reform, undertaken partly with the idea of working for the prevention of crime. They entertained, specifically, two basic conceptions— that, in order to improve the economic condition of the lower classes, reorganization of the system of poor relief was needed; and that a change should be made in the laws against vagabonds, whereby persons who were destitute, but not charged with any other offense, should be protected from arrest.[45]

More important than the efforts to secure these reforms, in which the Quakers labored jointly with others, was their agitation in behalf of the abolition of capital

---

by every possible encouragement to visit prisons, not merely to inspect them for the purpose of procuring information, but when the opportunity is afforded, to spend a certain portion of their time in habitual communication with those degraded but afflicted persons."

[45] Under the terms of 17 Geo. II. c. 5 and 32 Geo. III. c. 45, only vagabonds could receive an official pass, which would provide free transportation to their home community. People who were simply poor, but not declared vagabonds, were practically compelled to beg in order to gain the means of subsistence when traveling. Begging then resulted in their being committed to a house of correction.

punishment. Indeed, anyone, whether or not a member of the Society of Friends, who had visited the prisons [46] and offered consolation to the convicts just before their execution would have been moved to consideration of this question. But the Yearly Meeting took an official stand in the annual Epistles.[47] The hope, expressed in 1818, that as religion took a deeper hold on the nation, the popular demand for the abolition of capital punishment would gradually become too strong to be withstood, faded in the course of time; and in 1830 the wish was expressed that vigorous efforts might be made to influence Parliament through the coöperation of greater and greater numbers of persons with the individual Friends who were already active.

An Association for the Abolition of Capital Punishment, founded in 1808 and consisting principally of Quakers, the first association of this kind, had shown great zeal, directed at first toward the lessening of the severity of the law. A hopeful beginning was made; the number of capital crimes was diminished.[48] In 1830 a great popular movement was started to abolish the death penalty for forgery; the Quakers had secured the signatures of 1000 bankers from all over the country for a petition to Parliament.[49] In this special case, as for the whole problem, they laid special emphasis in their public debates upon the fact that the death penalty was ineffectual as a deterrent. At the beginning of the century barely 3 per cent of the

[46] See Richards, *op. cit.* (see note 26), p. 128.

[47] For instance, Yearly Meeting epistles for 1818, 1830, 1847.

[48] In 1828 a special organization was founded, the Association for Promoting Further Repeals of the Capital Statute.

[49] See also Allen's letter to the Duke of Wellington, 1830: Sherman, *op. cit.,* pp. 413-14; and *Memoir of Elizabeth Fry,* ii, 132.

sentences were actually carried out; the probability of execution for the individual criminal was therefore so slight that he hardly took it into account. Complete abolition moreover did not seem to be very dangerous, because in countries where it had been abolished there had been no increase in crime.[50]

It is well known that in England the movement has not attained its goal; it has nevertheless made considerable progress. The agitation of 1830 bore fruit two years later in an act of Parliament. And when Queen Victoria came to the throne in 1837, the number of capital crimes had diminished from 150 (the number at the beginning of the century) to ten.[51]

It is impossible to prove with certainty that direct influence of the Quaker reformers can be seen in all of the Parliamentary acts of those years which effected reorganization of prison administration in accord with ideas which they had expressed. Only the appointment of prison matrons, in 1824, and of prison overseers, in 1835, can be referred definitely to Elizabeth Fry. She had brought out the economic and moral value of women officials in women's prisons again and again, in many appeals to the authorities; their practical value had been brilliantly proved by the experiment at Newgate. On two occasions, in 1832 and in 1835, before the policy had been adopted of appointing prison inspectors, she had had opportunity to appear before a commission of the House

[50] William Tallack, *A General Review of the Subject of Capital Punishment*, published by the Society for the Abolition of Capital Punishment, in *Social Science Review*, New Series, No. 13, London January 2, 1865.
[51] Since 1861 murder and treason have been the only capital crimes in England.

of Commons as an expert and defend her opinions, gained through years of practical activity.

Permanent achievements of the friends of prisoners can be seen in foreign lands. Shillitoe, Allen, Buxton, the two Gurneys, and Elizabeth Fry had made opportunity during the course of many journeys through Europe to inspect the prisons almost everywhere. They had incorporated many a good idea, especially from the prisons of Holland, into their reform program; but they had much more often had occasion to appear before the authorities for the purpose of urging that existing abuses be remedied. Quaker principles were most completely realized in Germany, through the agency of the Rheinisch-Westfälische Gefängnisgesellschaft (Rhenish-Westphalian Prison Society), founded by Theodor Fliedner at Düsseldorf in 1826.[52]

Fliedner studied the activity of the British prison societies in London, and in so doing became personally acquainted with Elizabeth Fry;[53] her counsels regarding the care of prisoners in Germany preceded his coöperation in the organization of the English hospital system.[54] The Rhenish-Westphalian Prison Society, to which at present nine associations belong, has had a vigorous growth in the course of the years. The high esteem in which it is held is testified to by the assignment of special church collections to the furtherance of its aims. These

[52] See the *Memoir of Elizabeth Fry,* ii, 394; see also v. Rohden, *Geschichte der Rheinisch-Westfälischen Gefängnisgesellschaft* (History of the Rhenish-Westphalian Prison Society), Düsseldorf 1901.

[53] He writes of Elizabeth Fry: "No one of all my contemporaries has exercised such an influence upon my heart and life."

[54] See above, p. 151.

aims are defined as prevention of crime and the lessening of recidivism, or backsliding. Its activity consists, on the one hand, in combating drunkenness and prostitution, and, on the other hand, in the care of convicts during their term of imprisonment and after their discharge. It has established houses of refuge, asylums for victims of alcoholism, agricultural colonies for convicts, and institutions for the transition from prison back to normal life, especially for women prisoners; its numerous charitable societies find work for ex-convicts who have been discharged, and render them far-reaching aid in other ways.

In England there is no organization with an equally comprehensive program; yet there, too, the activity of the Quaker reformers has been continued along various lines. For in spite of all legal reform there is still a wide field of activity open to private individuals. The only remaining monument, to be sure, which specifically preserves the memory of the early friends of the convicts is a home for discharged women prisoners, the Elizabeth Fry Refuge; [55] but the larger organization, named in honor of Howard, [56] numbers many Quakers permanently among its members, and engages in various types of work very much in the Quaker spirit. Through its efforts to bring about centralization of English prison administration, and to organize a world-wide prison congress, this organization has striven to advance the science of penology; in addition it

[55] Founded in 1849 in memory of Elizabeth Fry, but having no connection with the Society of Friends.
[56] The Howard Association, founded in 1866. This Association publishes regularly the results of its investigations and reform proposals of all kinds, and its activity has often met with official recognition.

has attacked the housing problem, alcoholism, and other social ills, in order to remove some of the causes of crime. Thus the ground is gradually cleared for an approach to the ideal of criminal law, as the Quakers conceived it a hundred years ago: not punishment of the criminal, but prevention of the crime.

CHAPTER SIX

THE ABOLITION OF THE SLAVE TRADE
AND OF SLAVERY

JUST as the social reforms hitherto discussed were indebted to Quakers for their inception or continued prose-
cution, so the campaign against slavery, the fight of a
Christian point of view against important economic interests, owes its origin in part to the Society. The efforts of
the Friends in behalf of the slaves absorbed the greater
part of their energy through a number of decades, and
were better known than any of their other humanitarian
labors. The historical works on the subject, to be sure,
usually dismiss the services of the Quakers in this movement with but a few words; but their share in the abolition of the slave trade was recognized as early as 1808 by
Clarkson in his account of the progress of this first great
contest.[1] From his essay and the mass of material found
in the minutes, pamphlets, and journals of the time only
a relatively few details can be brought out within the limits of the present work.

As early as 1671 the founder of Quakerism issued
earnest appeals to all slaveholders among the Quakers in

[1] Thomas Clarkson, *History of the Rise, Progress, and Accomplishment
of the Abolition of the African Slave Trade by the British Parliament,*
London 1808, i, chs. 4 and 5.

Barbados to pay heed to the welfare of their helpless Negroes.[2] He demands kind treatment, protection from cruelty at the hands of the overseers, and emancipation after a certain number of years of service; and he lays upon the masters of slaves the duty of uplifting them by means of a strict Christian education; "for whom an account will be required by him who comes to judge both quick and dead, at the great day of judgment."[3]

In this demand Fox gave expression to an idea that was entirely new even to the Quakers; for until now the logical inference had not been drawn from their faith in all mankind, that even under a colored skin there was born a soul with an eternal destiny.[4] The relatively few Quakers among the settlers in the West Indies had presumably seen nothing wrong in the practice of the rest of the white people, but had availed themselves of slave labor without any consciousness of its essential injustice; and it cannot be proved that even Fox unconditionally condemned slavery as such. If he had done so, he would certainly have stepped forward with all his well-known zeal and militant vigor in behalf of its immediate abolition; but as a matter of fact he and his contemporaries contented themselves with preparing for reform in a thoroughly peaceful manner.

[2] Barbados was the first island of the West Indies to come into English possession. Quakers had been banished to this island and to Jamaica; and Fox visited them on his missionary journey.

[3] See *Journal*, ii, 149, 158. In 1675 William Edmundson preached to the Negroes and insisted, before the governor, that Christ had died for them as well as for other human beings.

[4] In the British Parliament Negroes were not recognized as human beings until 1790.

THE ABOLITION OF SLAVE TRADE AND SLAVERY

A defense against the accusation of the governor of Barbados, that the Quakers were stirring up the slaves to discontent and resistance, gives us an insight into their methods of work.[5] The sole purpose of the Friends was to impress upon the Negroes their obligations, arising from the teachings of Christianity, to their masters and to each other; to discourage violence, drunkenness, polygamy, and indeed any kind of vice; and to bring moral influences of all sorts to bear upon them. And throughout the next several decades their interest in the care of the Negroes expressed itself in small-scale work of this kind in Negro meetings, which Fox, down to the time of his death, adjured the missionary preachers to continue and to extend.[6] Such work constituted perhaps only a modest beginning; but it was no insignificant contribution to the whole movement, in view of the almost universal indifference to the plight of the slaves.

The denial of the ordinary rights of humanity to the slaves cannot be explained as a result of the well-known brutality of the period of the Restoration. Even the generation that devoted a not inconsiderable part of their energies through a number of decades to the establishment of the Kingdom of God on earth had sanctioned the slave trade. The first storm of protest against the English traders who imitated the example of the Spanish and Portuguese, in the time of Elizabeth, in acquiring West African Negroes for the slave market, had quickly subsided; and the public easily reconciled itself to the fact

[5] *Journal*, ii, 157-158.
[6] Epistle of December 11, 1690; Fox died January 13, 1691 (New Style). See *Journal*, ii, 502.

that a regular traffic in slaves grew up, under the protection of the government.[7]

In 1619 the first little band of Negroes was taken to certain English settlements in North America, and sold as laborers. The demand for this type of labor was soon established, and rose steadily; for even though the enslavement of natives captured in war was permitted, or the purchase of members of other races as slaves, these methods were not nearly sufficient to meet the demand. After the Restoration the English government granted to the Royal African Society, at the head of which stood the Duke of York, a monopoly in the importation of Negroes into British colonies. At about the same time various acts were passed confirming the status of the Negroes as outside the protection of the law.[8]

To be sure, many free-born Englishmen were in as sorry a plight as if they had been slaves. The deportation of prisoners of war, convicts, and other objectionable elements of society, who were hired out as slaves upon their arrival in the foreign country, had not even been stopped under Cromwell.[9] Persons who wished to emi-

[7] George Jellinek, *The Declaration of the Rights of Man and of Citizens* (translated by Max Farrand from the German, *Die Erklärung der Menschen- und Bürgerrechte*), New York 1901, p. 57: "The natural freedom of man was set forth by many writers during the eighteenth century as compatible with lawful servitude. Even Locke, for whom liberty forms the very essence of man, in his *Fundamental Constitutions for Carolina,* sanctioned slavery and servitude."

[8] Civilian rights were even denied to free Negroes; all children of slave women were declared to be slaves; the killing of a negro was not considered murder, etc.

[9] In 1619, for instance, a load of 100 prostitutes was sent off to Virginia; all in all, about 2,000 persons were deported each year, in order that the home country might be rid of them and might be saved the cost of maintaining them in prison. See Alfred Zimmermann, *Kolonialpolitik* (Colonial policies), Series 1, No. 18 of *Hand- und Lehrbuch der Staats-*

grate but were without money were accustomed to bind themselves as servants (the so-called "redemptioners"), in order to earn their passage money.

Negro slavery seemed to be something analogous, because the fact was overlooked that the capture of Negroes could not be justified as punishment for any crime, nor could their submission to slavery be considered in any wise a voluntary act. On the contrary, the Negroes were forcibly seized, and carried off without the shadow of a legal right.[10] The wrongs of the Negroes were further aggravated by the fact that, in contrast to the patriarchal system extant in the Spanish and Portuguese colonies, the practice in the English colonies was to drive the slaves with notorious severity. This was the result perhaps of a certain economic stress which the colonists had begun to feel when their profits were cut down by the Navigation Acts and later additions to them.

Though the statements just made apply only to the plantations of the Southern colonies, the North had not been able to keep its skirts clear of slaveholding. The colonial frontier needed population; it was often impossible, in spite of vigorous efforts, to secure white labor.[11] Negroes, on the other hand, were easy to get. Such causes may well explain the existence of slaveholding in Pennsyl-

---

wissenschaften (Handbook and textbook of political science), Leipzig 1905, p. 176. In 1664 banishment to the West Indies was introduced as punishment for vagabonds and religious nonconformists, in 1678 for those convicted of political crimes.

[10] Occasional references to this point, as in a protest by Richard Baxter (Friends' Reference Library, Tract volume 331), had no effect whatever.

[11] On account of the complaints of English industry and agriculture, there were repeated Parliamentary acts prohibiting emigration; e.g., in 1686, 1719, etc.

THE QUAKERS AS PIONEERS

vania, and the fact that Penn, though very much troubled, took no steps against it. A provision was made, to be sure, in the statutes of the Free Society of Traders, in 1682, that Negroes were to be set free after a fourteen-year term of service; but it seems doubtful whether this regulation was ever carried out—indeed, whether it was even applied to Penn's own slaves. However, though the antislavery movement did not originate with Penn, it started within the Society of Friends, and in his community, and was destined in time to become a prime force in the abolition of this great social evil.

The credit of being the first to recognize the incompatibility of slaveholding with the Quaker teachings belongs to a group of German settlers. We refer to the inhabitants of Germantown, colonists[12] from Krefeld, Frankfurt, and Kirchheim (in the Palatinate), who were induced to emigrate by Penn on his missionary journeys in Germany and by his report of Pennsylvania, which was widely circulated in a German translation.[13]

The leader of these German settlers was Francis Daniel Pastorius, a jurist of good family, highly educated and yet of deep religious feeling, who felt driven to forgo a brilliant career in order to become teacher and preacher to the American colonists.[14] There is preserved

[12] Originally they were Mennonites or Pietists.

[13] The ravaging of the Palatinate in 1674 and 1688 may have given additional impetus to the emigration to America.

[14] See Marion Dexter Learned, *The Life of Francis Daniel Pastorius, the Founder of Germantown*, Philadelphia, 1908. Pastorius was the precursor of the French Encyclopedists, through his book *Bee Hive*, which is called the "Magna Charta of German culture in colonial America," and the "speculum scientiarum" (mirror of the sciences) of the seventeenth century. For further information on Pastorius see C. B. Hylkema, *Reformateurs* . . . (see above, p. 24), ii, 209-210.

in his handwriting the first public protest against negro slavery, a letter presented to a meeting at Germantown, Pennsylvania, held Second Month [April] 18, 1688, and forwarded to a monthly meeting held at Dublin, Bucks County, Second Month [April] 30, 1688.[15]

In this letter primary emphasis is laid upon religious and moral arguments against slavery. The difficult injunction, "do unto others as ye would that they should do unto you," we are told, is grossly disregarded. Reference is made to the general fear of pirates, who made prisoners of travelers in order to sell them into slavery.[16] Such conduct is ordinarily bitterly condemned even when the Turks are the ones guilty of it; how much greater is the sin when Christians steal human beings! The black color of the skin of the victims does not serve as an excuse; for individual and personal freedom is a natural corollary of the universal freedom of conscience which Pennsylvania has assumed as an inalienable right. And besides, it is obviously unrighteous to acquire persons who have been kidnaped, and thus to sanction theft. Further, it is not right to continue causing the seventh commandment to be disregarded, by breaking up the natural family ties of the Negroes and bringing together those already married in new combinations. Finally, there are practical considerations in favor of giving up slavery, says the letter. The Quakers will acquire a bad reputation in Europe

[15] For reprint of Pastorius's letter see S. W. Pennypacker, *The Settlement of Germantown*, Philadelphia 1899, p. 145ff.; see also Learned, *op. cit.*, pp. 261, 262.

[16] There was a widespread fear of pirates at this time. Quakers had repeatedly fallen into captivity in Algier; suits to secure their release, and collections for ransom, occupied the Meeting for Sufferings repeatedly during the seventies and eighties of the seventeenth century.

if the report goes abroad that they buy and sell
human beings like cattle; and this will discourage emigration.

The Monthly Meeting recognized the importance of this
communication, but did not feel that the decision of such
a question lay within its jurisdiction, and referred it to the
Quarterly Meeting.[17] The Quarterly Meeting also hesitated to take a definite stand, and so, on September 5,
1688, the protest came before the Yearly Meeting in Burlington. The Yearly Meeting in its turn suspended judgment for the time being, "it having so General a Relation
to many other Parts, and, therefore at present they
forbear It." [18]

But though the concern of the Germans did not result
in official action at this time, the question had once for all
been squarely put, and continued to occupy men's minds.
By 1693 we find the counsel extended to Friends to buy
slaves only for the purpose of setting them free; and
three years later the Yearly Meeting lays it upon the
consciences of its members not to do anything to encourage the further importation of Negroes,[19] to bring those
already in their possession to meeting, and to care for

[17] "We having inspected ye matter above mentioned & considered of it,
we finde it so weighty that we think it not Expedient for vs to meddle
with it here, but do Rather comit it to ye consideration of ye Quarterly
meeting; ye tennor of it being nearly Related to ye Truth." Learned,
op. cit., p. 262.

[18] Learned, *op. cit.,* p. 263.

[19] Economic conditions were not very well adapted to slavery; industry
was based primarily on the export trade, especially of firewood. Legal
regulations restricted the development of trade: clothing and household
furniture had to be imported from England. See David Macpherson,
Annals of Commerce, Manufactures, Fisheries, and Navigation, London
1805, iii, 188 and iv, 393.

them kindly in every way.[20] This proposal, to be sure, did not find much favor.

The Proprietor of Pennsylvania was apparently in advance of the organized body of his fellow believers in regard to the treatment of Negro slaves. William Penn showed an active interest in their status, and expressed the hope that their legal rights might be regulated and they themselves, through proper influence upon their morals, educated to a higher level of life, so that in the course of time an equality between the black and white races might be possible; but in spite of this desire, the Society adopted a negative attitude, and the antislavery agitation made no progress for a number of years. From 1705 on—Penn had meanwhile gone back to England to represent the interests of the Colony during the War of the Spanish Succession, and does not appear to have exercised further influence on the course pursued by the Society—the Yearly Meeting rose to the point of definite action on several occasions, inducing the Assembly to lay a tariff upon the importation of Negroes, and, in 1711, even to prohibit such importations altogether. This law, however, did not receive the necessary confirmation from the British crown,[21] since both Houses of Parliament considered the slave trade advantageous to England and the colonies. Also a law passed by the Quaker colony in 1714, which imposed an import duty of £20 for each

[20] Allen C. Thomas and Richard H. Thomas, *History of the Society of Friends in America,* 6th edition Philadelphia 1930, p. 114.

[21] The laws passed in Pennsylvania had to be submitted to the Privy Council within five years after their enactment; and the British king could veto them within six months thereafter. After the lapse of this time the crown had no power of veto. Macpherson, *op. cit.,* iii, 187.

Negro imported, was vetoed by the Queen. This was all too easy to understand, since the Assiento Treaty had meanwhile made England the greatest slave trader in the world.[22] Under these conditions the Quakers had no means of using compulsion; and the feeling of individual responsibility, which might have replaced a rigid regulation of this kind, seems not yet to have been developed. The repeated statements issued by the London Yearly Meeting with respect to the slave trade (e.g., in 1713, 1715, 1727) received scant consideration in the colonies; and in the American meetings the condemnation of slavery for the time being was considerably milder than in England.[23]

Not until 1743, when a study was made of the part the Quakers were playing in the slave trade, were any energetic measures undertaken. Following the publication of the private investigations of individual members, principally of Benezet [24] and Woolman,[25] which brought

[22] By the Peace of Utrecht in 1713, the Assiento (that is, the right of supplying the colonies with Negroes) was renounced by Spain in favor of England. England had assumed the obligation of shipping 4800 Negroes a year to the Spanish colonies for a period of thirty years, but had also the right to import as many more Negroes as she might choose, at a reduced import duty—$33.50 apiece for the first 4800 Negroes, half this amount for any number above 4800. Before the end of the thirty-year period, however, the treaty was terminated because of the disputes to which it led.

[23] Thus the Chester Meeting asked that all Friends should avoid as much as possible the buying and selling of Negroes, in order not to provoke the members who might be present; but the note is expressly added: "This is only caution, not censure."

[24] Anthony Benezet (1713-1784), of a respected Huguenot family which migrated to Pennsylvania in 1731. Benezet was a teacher, and took part in many movements in the interests of the poor, the unemployed, and the sick; he worked for the abolition of the duel, opposed the unintelligent treatment of the insane, and took an interest in the Indians. From 1776 on he devoted himself to the abolition of slavery.

[25] John Woolman (1720-1772), employed in a modest position in busi-

grave abuses to light in the slave trade,[26] there was issued in 1754 an earnest exhortation to members to set their slaves free; and in 1758 the Philadelphia Yearly Meeting determined to exclude all owners of slaves from the meetings for discipline, but not without renewed efforts to induce them to give up their slaveholding. A delegation with Woolman at its head was sent out to visit all slaveholders. Woolman's Journal gives some interesting pictures of the difficulties of their task.[27]

In spite of widespread recognition of the unproductivity of slave labor, the lack of other labor led to the continued use of Negroes, because people would no longer be satisfied with the modest livelihood they could earn by their own industry. Material interests played a not inconsiderable rôle at this time in the colonies just as in the mother country, although the Yearly Meetings on both sides of the Atlantic fought against the power of worldly considerations.[28] When it appeared that the slave trade, arising from the "filthy covetousness" of the members of the Society, was increasingly causing the breakdown of

---

ness in West Jersey (at Burlington and Mt. Holly, in what is now called New Jersey), and hence often forced to witness the purchase and sale of slaves. During his later period of activity he tried to bring about the abolition of slavery.

[26] Mention should also be made of Benjamin Lay (1677-1759), who published a protest against the slave trade as early as 1737, and stirred up many people through his enthusiasm. He seems however to have accomplished but little, as he was a somewhat peculiar person.

[27] See *The Journal and Essays of John Woolman,* edited by Amelia Mott Gummere, London 1922, pp. 58ff. and 215ff.

[28] See for instance the Philadelphia Yearly Meeting Minutes of 1757, 1758, 1761, and 1763, and the Yearly Meeting Epistles of 1758 and 1763. John Griffith writes in his *Journal,* London 1779, p. 380: "It is too manifest to be denied that the life of religion is almost lost, where slaves are very numerous; and it is impossible it should be otherwise, the practice being as contrary to the spirit of Christianity, as light is to darkness."

their simple habits and strict religious training, and endangering their holiest principles, the London Yearly Meeting in 1761 took the decisive step, and issued the order that all slave owners and slave traders should be expelled from the Society. Two years later even assistance rendered to the practice of slavery was declared punishable.

Naturally, such action on the part of the London Yearly Meeting could not improve conditions in the colonies over night. The results in America, however, seem to have been as good as could be expected, for the Epistle of 1772 expresses satisfaction at the great decrease in slavery. The Quakers had not the power at this time to effect the complete abolition of slavery, for in the Southern colonies it was forbidden by law to set slaves free except under special conditions.[29] Instead of using this fact as an excuse for inactivity, the Friends who lived in that part of the country attempted to have these restrictions removed. Their meeting addressed a petition to the King in 1772; and the negative answer which it received was one of the causes, according to Clarkson, for the revolt of the Colonies a few years later.

The American Revolution had the effect of removing the Quakers, as opponents of war, from participation in the administration of government, and the effective coöperation of English and American Quakers for active propaganda in England was thereby interfered with; but the antislavery movement in America suffered no check.

[29] Emancipation was permitted only for the cause of some conspicuous service rendered, and when specially authorized by an act of the governor and assembly.

THE ABOLITION OF SLAVE TRADE AND SLAVERY

The freeing of slaves, and the care of those who had been freed, made gratifying progress, not only among Friends but among members of other faiths.[30]

Even earlier than this, in 1770, little antislavery societies had been formed, under the leadership of Quakers, in various parts of the middle provinces of North America, to which belonged members of the English Established Church, Presbyterians, and Catholics; the first permanent organization of all friends of the slaves occurred in 1774 as a result of the efforts of the Quaker James Pemberton and of a distinguished citizen, Dr. Benjamin Rush, representing the non-Quakers. The purpose of this organization was "to promote the emancipation of the slaves, and to assist free Negroes who were unjustly kept in bondage." Its headquarters were in Pennsylvania, but it set up numerous branches during the eighties, and soon entered into correspondence with persons in England who were sincerely interested. In connection with the contacts of the society with English Friends, special mention should be made of an English pamphleteer and scholar, Granville Sharp (1735-1813); for he had published an essay in 1769 on the injustice and the dangers of slavery in England,[31] and after endless difficulty had brought

[30] Epistle of 1774: "Our testimony against the inhuman practice of slave keeping gains ground and hath had some happy influence on the minds of considerate people of other denominations"; and Epistle of 1777: "The Christian endeavours and example of our brethren in this respect afford an additional satisfaction, as they have induced many of other professions to restore numbers of these injured people to their liberty."

[31] *A Representation of the Injustice and dangerous Tendency of tolerating Slavery in England.* Friends' Reference Library, Tract vol. 331, p. 141ff.

about the enactment of a law to the effect "that as soon as any slave sets his foot upon English territory, he becomes free." [32] (See article on Granville Sharp, in *Dictionary of National Biography*.)

The first attempt on the part of the Quakers to effect changes in English law in the interests of slaves dates from 1783. Their petition to the House of Commons [33] is the first memorial that was ever presented to Parliament on this subject. It is clear from this document that they were moved to take this step by religious considerations, and that they had been confirmed in their attitude by the abundant opportunity they had had to observe the operation of slavery at first hand. The indifference of people to the question appears to them to be partly explainable by their relatively slight acquaintance with the actual facts; but a Christian nation, in their view, cannot afford to countenance a practice that is as contrary to humanity and justice as is the institution of slavery. The necessity of legislative interference is based not exclusively on ethical considerations; with the Quakers' characteristic alignment of their theories with economic fact, the petition points out that the development of Africa, from which England would derive more profit than any other country, would be checked by the export of Negroes.

The reading of this petition in Parliament elicited some

---

[32] This law applied only to slaves that were brought to England by their masters. The attempts of such slaves to gain their freedom, and the pursuit of those who escaped, often had extremely unpleasant consequences.

[33] *The Case of our Fellow Creatures, the Oppressed Africans, respectfully recommended to the Serious Consideration of the Legislature of Great Britain by the People called Quakers*. See Rufus M. Jones, *The Later Periods of Quakerism*, London 1921, i, pp. 321, 322.

THE ABOLITION OF SLAVE TRADE AND SLAVERY

applause; but because the session was far advanced the
subject could not receive full discussion.[34] It served as
the starting point in Europe for Quaker propaganda on
a large scale. The same Yearly Meeting which had
decided to send the petition to the House of Commons
instructed its standing committee (the Meeting for Sufferings) to present a memorial to the King and to the
House of Lords, and to attempt to inform influential persons as to the evils of the slave trade. During the next
several years the Yearly Meeting considered ways and
means for bringing about the abolition of slavery as part
of its regular program of business. In 1784 a wide distribution of pamphlets was undertaken explaining the
Quaker point of view; and further data were collected.
At the same time the Quakers contributed articles on
slavery to the most important papers of London and
other large cities, in order to spread a knowledge of its
evils as widely as possible.

A few of the arguments advanced may be recapitulated
from the collection of these writings still extant.[35] The
early protests repeat the ideas brought out by Fox and the
first American Quaker meetings, without explaining the
origin of slavery or considering rationally the possibility

[34] This petition, as the first to be presented on the Negro question,
attracted a good deal of attention from the public as well as in Parliament. Thus the *Morning Chronicle* reports (June 1783): "Sir Cecil Wray
called the attention of the House to a matter in which he said their
humanity was much interested; it being no other than an appeal to their
feelings as men and as Christians in behalf of a great number of their
fellow creatures, the Negroes whom they kept in Slavery. . . . The advanced period of the sessions rendered it utterly impossible to comply
with the prayer of a Petition coming from *the most humane religious sect
in the Christian World.* The petition was ordered to lie on the table."
[35] *Tracts on the Slave Trade,* Friends' Reference Library, Tract vol.
331.

of its abolition.[36] Other pamphlets go more deeply into
the matter: they give a history of slavery,[37] and make
some attempt to answer the arguments advanced in its
defense, as for instance the alleged inability of white
persons to work in hot climates. Thus it is shown that in
Barbados white laborers had once cultivated the fields and
worked ten hours a day, and that the white population
had gradually degenerated after the introduction of
Negroes, as a consequence of laziness, excesses, and various resulting sicknesses, so that a real need was now felt
for black labor, though a gain in productivity at least
could be secured by setting the blacks free.

Benezet made some especially interesting studies on
the condition of the Negroes in Africa and on the methods of the slave traders.[38] The Negroes are described as
being altogether kindly, and, in their native land, peaceful
and intelligent. It was not until they came into contact
with the Europeans that, as a natural consequence of the
treatment they received, they developed certain bad characteristics, as a tendency to deception and the like. For
the slave traders organized regular slave hunts, or incited
the Negroes to war with each other, in order to be able to
buy the captives.

From other essays it is apparent that the process of
forcible reduction to slavery involved a fearful waste of

[36] For instance, Elihu Coleman, *A Testimony against the Antichristian
Practice of Making Slaves of Men*, 1733.
[37] *Two Dialogues on the Man Trade*, printed in London 1760.
[38] *A Short Account of that Part of Africa, inhabited by the Negroes*,
Philadelphia 1762; also, *A Caution and Warning to Great Britain and
her Colonies, in a Short Representation of the Calamitous state of the
enslaved Negroes in the British Dominions*. Collected from various
Authors and Submitted to the Serious Consideration of all, more especially of those in Power, Philadelphia 1766.

human life. Of the 100,000 Negroes brought into the British colonies annually, a third died within the first year."

The Quakers were now entirely agreed that radical reform was necessary, and the following specific measures were proposed: absolute prohibition of further importation of slaves; emancipation of all present slaves as soon as their purchase price or the cost of their training could be considered to have been met;⁴⁰ and the settling of these freed slaves in the colonies, where they were to maintain themselves by cultivating their own farms or by selling their labor to whites. The plantation owners affected by these measures could be reimbursed, if necessary, from public funds; and the work of emancipation should proceed regardless of alleged injury to trade, i.e., in sugar and tobacco.⁴¹

These were the principal points made in the more important Quaker writings, which constituted only a part of the total literature published by members of the Society on the slavery question. Other persons, not members, were drawn into propagandist activity, in accord-

[39] These figures refer to the year 1753. In 1788 an investigation conducted under the authority of Parliament brought out the fact that, if 25% of the Negroes imported in any one year were still alive three years later, conditions were considered to be unusually good.

[40] A lengthening of the term of slavery was to be brought about only through intentional carelessness in service.

[41] It seems to have been assumed, though it was never proved, that emancipation would actually cause such injury to trade. It was further assumed that sugar could be produced in Africa more cheaply than in the British colonies, unless slave labor could be utilized by British growers. It was thought that African sugar would be cheaper than that from the French colonies, which at that time were able to underbid England in the foreign markets, the ratio of prices being 25:16. See James Ramsay, *Enquiry into the Effects of putting a stop to the Slave Trade,* London 1784.

ance with the general aim of the Friends, to strengthen any move for the common good by securing the coöperation of others. Thus in 1785 they arranged for the translation and distribution of a prize essay [42] written at the University of Cambridge, the author of which, Thomas Clarkson,[43] though engaged in preparing himself for the church as a profession, soon made the decision to devote his powers entirely to the agitation against slavery. Through the efforts of this man, who had many contacts with members of Parliament, clergymen, and other persons in high positions, a union of the various groups of the opponents of slavery was finally brought about, and an effective campaign made possible. On May 22, 1787, a committee was formed consisting of twelve men (only three of whom were non-Quakers: Clarkson, Granville Sharp, and Philip Sansom), who, with William Wilberforce to lead the cause in Parliament, carried on a stiff fight for the abolition of the slave trade during the next twenty years and brought it to a victorious conclusion.[44]

After the Quakers had begun publicly to urge the emancipation of all slaves, they were obliged to take particular pains to see that no one within their membership was chargeable with a practice which the Society as a whole officially condemned; for otherwise a welcome opportunity would have been offered to numerous opponents

[42] *Anne liceat invitos in servitutem dare?* (Is it right to reduce persons to slavery against their will?)

[43] The author of the above-mentioned *History . . . of the Abolition of the African Slave Trade* . . . (see above, note 1, p. 197).

[44] See Clarkson, *op. cit.* (see above, note 1), i, 257, and H. F. Uhden, *Leben des William Wilberforce* (Life of W. W.), Berlin 1840.

to attack them.[45] At the beginning of the seventies there
were probably only a few scattering cases left in Great
Britain. In America, complete abolition of slavery had
been attained as early as 1774 in Pennsylvania, by 1782
in the jurisdiction of the New England Yearly Meeting,
by 1787 even in the South; so that in this year there was
not a single slave in the possession of a member of the
Society of Friends.[46]

With this the Quaker movement in behalf of the
Negroes enters a new stage; within the meetings there remained from now on only the problem of caring for freedmen. Their success in solving this problem determined in
some measure the effectiveness of their public propaganda; for it supplied the defense against many of the
attacks that were made upon the proposal to abolish
slavery. Of these there was no lack. Before the opening
of Parliament, in 1788, the Lower House received 103
petitions [47] from "friends of the unfortunate Africans,"
and the slavery question was therefore taken up for con-

[45] Thus a passage in the London Yearly Meeting Epistle of 1784
reads: "It is our earnest desire, that none under our name may weaken
or counteract our endeavours by contributing, in any way, to the support
of this iniquitous commerce."

[46] The dates are from Whittier's introduction to the *Journal* of John
Woolman, London 1900, p. 20ff., and *Memoir of Anthony Benezet,* by Rob-
erts Vaux (2d edition, revised by Wilson Armistead, London 1859), pp. 72,
73, which quotes Clarkson, *op. cit.,* i, 179. The sources differ in the
matter of dates. Thus John Fiske, *The Dutch and Quaker Colonies in
America,* ii, 326, says: "In 1776 a declaration of independence for all
slaves held by Friends was decreed." According to the Minutes another
general inquiry was authorized in the year 1784, as to whether there
were still members who were "not wholly clear"; and against any such,
steps were to be taken.

[47] Many of these had been sent by cities as a result of Quaker
activity.

sideration; but as soon as the deliberations began, numerous counter petitions of the slave traders were received.[48] The position of these latter was strengthened by the fact that a royal commission, which was supposed to examine the slavery question from all angles, came to the conclusion that most of the indictments pronounced against the slave trade were without foundation—a judgment which is all the more unintelligible as the report contains references to many specific incidents which the publications of the Quakers completely confirmed.

The Lower House thereupon determined to institute a further inquiry into this matter, but in the meantime directed its immediate attention toward securing a certain degree of regulation of the slave trade. Through the untiring investigations of Clarkson and a few Quakers, who had inspected the slave ships in English ports, especially Bristol, and had gathered information of all kinds, the terrible plight had been exposed not only of the Negroes who were being transported,[49] but also of the English sailors.[50] The result was that the necessity of immediate interference by the government seemed so obvious as to be beyond dispute.

With reference to the abolition of slavery, the question arose for discussion as to whether it lay within the juris-

[48] See Macpherson, *op. cit.*, iv, 141. The opponents of abolition published various essays, including a pamphlet by R. Harris, *Scriptural Researches on the Licitness of the Slave-Trade*, 1788.

[49] Clarkson collected, among other things, samples of the fetters and the instruments of torture that were used.

[50] It was shown that 50% of the crews deserted or died. Pitt observed: "The slave trade, instead of being a nursery to English seamen, was their grave; more seamen died in the slave trade in one year than in the whole remaining trade in two."

diction of England to interfere with the internal affairs of the colonies, or whether such matters should be determined by the corporate governments already locally established. The British Parliament had exclusive authority to regulate all branches of trade between England and her colonies, including of course the slave trade; but trade between the colonies, or slaveholding within the colonies, might be considered a different matter. In view of considerations of this sort the above-mentioned committee [51] had determined, even before the opening of the Parliament, to devote its efforts at first to the abolition of commerce in slaves.[52] It was argued that, if the importation of slaves was stopped, better treatment of the slaves would follow of its own accord, for the welfare and natural increase of the slaves would then be a matter of personal interest to their masters. And, if importation could not be directly stopped, the establishment of standardized conditions for the transportation of Negroes might serve as an important step in the direction of the abolition of the trade, the more especially if the maximum number of slaves allowed for each ship were so diminished that slave transportation could no longer be carried on at a profit.

The law of 1788 did not accomplish this end. It did, however, at least prevent any such increase in the export of slaves from Africa as might naturally have resulted from the expectation that the slave trade would soon be stopped altogether; and it prevented also the lowering

[51] See p. 214.
[52] From now on the organization which this committee represented was therefore called the Society for the Abolition of the Slave Trade.

of the standards which would have gone hand in hand with such increase.[53] In other ways also the law had effects which were not without significance.

The debates in Parliament aroused much more public interest in the question than all the propaganda. In the words of Clarkson, they "had produced a kind of holy flame, or enthusiasm, and this to a degree and to an extent never before witnessed."[54] No better evidence could be found of the sincerity of the abolitionists than the fact that, disregarding all the barriers raised by their different religious affiliations, members of the Established Church worked hand in hand with dissenters. Even bishops allied themselves with the modest Society (*i.e.*, for the Abolition of the Slave Trade), which consisted for the most part of Quakers.[55] The labors of this Society had greatly expanded even during the session of Parliament, and kept on increasing; and the number of members grew in proportion. Branch associations were formed in England and on the Continent[56] to attempt to see to it that the slave trade should not be continued by other nations, or, on account of possible gain, taken up by nations not

[53] Attempts were made to improve conditions by offering premiums to the captains and doctors of ships on which the mortality during the journey did not amount to more than two or three per cent.

[54] Clarkson, *History* . . ., i, 572.

[55] The official attitude adopted by the Yearly Meeting of 1788 brought about this condition. The Epistle reads, in part: "The increasing solicitude for the suppression of the slave-trade, which appears among all ranks of people, is cause of thankfulness to the common Father of mankind, and encourages us to hope, that the time is approaching when this nation will be cleansed from that defilement. Let us, in the meantime, continue, with unabating ardour, to be intercessors for the greatly injured Africans."

[56] The Paris organization bore the name "Friends of the Negroes"; La Rochefoucauld, Lafayette, and Condorcet were members.

hitherto engaged in it, as soon as England should abandon it.

The English Society continued to distribute pamphlets explaining their point of view by tens of thousands,[57] held meetings, and established contacts with ships' doctors and other persons, in order to have witnesses ready when the slavery question should next come up in Parliament. This latter point was a matter of greater difficulty for the abolitionists than for their opponents; for whoever testified as an expert in the matter of cargoes and overloading usually contributed thereby to his own material loss, whereas the defenders of the status quo could find an abundance of helpers who would testify with the opposite motive.

The great hearings at which witnesses presented both sides of the question took place before a special commission of Parliament from 1789 to 1791. The arguments of the abolitionists were confirmed in these hearings, and new arguments were developed;[58] but the contentions of the other side also [59] met with effective support from gov-

[57] The abolitionists also worked out plans of the slave ships, in order to give a clear realization of how terrible the overcrowding was. It was shown that the passengers had not room enough to lie down at full length alongside one another, and that the distance between decks was not great enough to enable them to stand upright. "On the slave ships living men had less room than corpses usually have in their coffins."

[58] *Abstract of Evidence delivered before a select Committee of the House of Commons in the years 1790-91 on the Part of the Petitioners for the Abolition of the Slave-Trade,* printed in 1791.

[59] *A Summary of Evidence before the Committee of the Privy Council and of the House of Commons.* (Friends' Reference Library, Tracts H II.) There were four points that received primary consideration: the inability of white persons to work on the plantations of the West Indies; the impossibility of maintaining the existing number of Negroes unimpaired without importing them; the futility of the abandonment of the slave trade by England, since it would be taken up by other nations; and the value of the slave trade to the English navy.

ernors of the colonies and from admirals; and the result was that Wilberforce's proposal was defeated even in the Lower House.

This defeat was partly counterbalanced by the agreement to found the so-called Sierra Leone Company (at first for a period of thirty-one years), for the colonization of a part of the African coast. In this enterprise free labor alone was to be used.[60] The plan provided that schools should be established in Sierra Leone, the industry of the natives stimulated in every possible way, and an export and an import trade developed. We may anticipate the story by saying here that this undertaking was an experiment of great significance in the history of civilization, especially because of the stimulus it afforded for the establishment of other organizations with like aims; [61] but it had to weather various severe economic crises, principally because of hostile encroachments of the French.

The postponement of a thoroughgoing regulation of the slave trade by law had the effect of strengthening the position of the abolitionists; yet even the great enthusiasm of the year 1792—in which, according to Macpherson, 519 petitions from clerical and temporal corpor-

[60] Preliminary steps for such a project had been taken some years before. In 1787, great numbers of Negroes had been freed by the War with the American colonies and, being without work or any means of support, had flooded London, and brought great distress upon themselves and others. In this emergency, a group of charitably disposed persons had arranged to have them transported to Sierra Leone. The experiment met with little success, because shiftlessness, laziness, sickness, and general demoralization led to numerous desertions. Moreover, along with this Negro transport the British authorities got rid of a number of persons of ill repute, principally prostitutes, whose presence must have had unfavorable effects. See Macpherson, *op. cit.*, iv, 127. The renewed attempt, however, showed that the plan was not considered hopeless.

[61] For instance, the Society for the Purpose of Cultivating the Tropical Productions by the hired Labour of the Free Natives.

ations of England and Scotland were received by Parliament—did not suffice to rout the opponents of abolition. Attempts to destroy the slave trade by boycotting articles manufactured by slave labor were also unsuccessful. Following the example which had been set by the American Quakers ever since 1770, the British began in 1791 to form associations of friends of the Negroes all over the country, the members of which pledged themselves to give up the use of sugar as long as slave labor was used in growing it; but the spirit of self-sacrifice did not last long enough, or extend widely enough, to have any practical results.

In the course of the next few years the abolitionists met with some small degree of success in America. A petition of the Quakers to the federal government of the United States resulted in 1794 in an act which prohibited the export of slaves, thus giving grounds for hope that further change in the law would be made. The London annual Epistle of 1795 expresses joyful satisfaction over the news, and praises the efforts of the American meetings, which were educating Negro children to be useful members of society.[62] Such education was regarded in the light of a special obligation, since slave labor had contributed so largely to the colonization of the country.

The progress made by English Quakers within the next few years, and by abolitionists in general, can be briefly indicated. In 1798 the Society of Friends handed in a

[62] Benezet, who had had very good results in an evening school for slaves, had come to the conclusion as a result of his experience that the alleged mental and spiritual inferiority of the Negroes should be emphatically denied.

third petition to Parliament, of essentially the same content as the earlier ones, and did not allow themselves to be discouraged by a third failure. In the Epistle of this year emphasis is laid on the statement that nothing should prevent the Quakers from acting as public defenders of the slaves. In 1799 the regulations governing slave transportation were made materially more exacting; and after the turn of the century the question was finally settled in favor of the oppressed race. The acts of 1805 and 1806 [63] were the forerunners of the Abolition Bill, which received the royal signature on March 25, 1807. By the terms of this bill the departure of slave ships from English harbors was prohibited after the first of May, and their entrance into ports in the colonies was prohibited after the first of March of the following year.

Thus the long desired goal was finally attained, and complete eradication of commerce in human beings appeared to be near at hand, since the United States prohibited the import of slaves at about the same time. [64] The biographies of the individual fighters in the cause, as well as the official Epistle of the Yearly Meeting of 1807, give a picture of the rejoicing and thankfulness of the Quakers. But, in spite of their past efforts, they did not rest here; the abolitionists were confronted by many new tasks. For the cessation of marine slave trade was only the first step

[63] The act of 1805 prohibited the importation of slaves by British traders into the colonies conquered by England during the war; the act of 1806 prohibited the transportation of slaves into foreign countries, the traffic in slaves by means of foreign ships, and the outfitting of foreign slave ships in English ports. An additional clause prohibited the use of ships for the slave trade unless they had previously been used for that purpose.

[64] By the law of March 2, 1807, effective January 1, 1808.

toward the total abolition of slavery, to which they now
turned their attention with increased zeal.

The first evidence of this new campaign was the establishment of the African Institution, an association for the
civilizing of Africa and the eradication of surreptitious
slave trading, founded through the initiative of the
Quaker William Allen. The association aimed also to
further the sale of African products, to elevate the natives
by means of education, and in general to show sympathy
for them in every possible way.[65] Much good was accomplished, though the complete realization of the program
was prevented by various untoward circumstances: it was
commonly believed that the association, of which the
Duke of Gloucester was the president, and which num-
bered many members from among the highest social circles, failed because of its very nobility.[66] Nevertheless,
the association deserves credit for having shown other
humane persons the way to a field where labor would be
richly blessed. But more of that later; for the present we
are considering the Quaker activities of 1807.

The slavery question had drawn the Friends, who were
fundamentally a nonpolitical organization, more and
more into participation in political life. If they could not
themselves plead the cause of the slaves in Parliament,
they could at least work for the election of candidates who
were of their way of thinking. In 1807 especially, a lively
campaign was waged to secure Wilberforce's reëlection.
In York the meeting urged its members to do all pos-

[65] See James Sherman, *Memoir of William Allen,* Philadelphia [1851],
pp. 53-54 and 73-80.
[66] Henry Richard, *Memoirs of Joseph Sturge,* London 1864, p. 78: "It
died of its own dignity."

sible,[67] both by personal coöperation and by liberal contributions; and the Quakers deluged the voters with numerous illustrated broadsides, on which the sufferings of the slaves were represented, in order to create a sentiment against the defenders of slavery.

Not only were the abolitionists obliged to fight against slavery as such, but renewed efforts were needed against slave trading, as it soon became apparent that the law of 1807 proved to be entirely ineffective in preventing the trade. Aside from the fact that slave traders were often able to elude discovery altogether, they were quite willing to risk a punishment amounting at the worst to a money fine which was less than the profit from a successful trip. In 1811 and 1819 acts were passed declaring that slave trading constituted a felony punishable with transportation; and attempts were made, beginning at the Congress of Vienna, to bring about international agreements for the complete abolition of slavery; but these results indicated only apparent success on the part of the abolitionists. Investigations made by the Quakers in the early twenties,[68] and communications from the African Institution, proved that the barbarous trade persisted in spite of legal prohibition. Spanish and Portuguese traders, to be sure, were the principal participants; but there was no lack of English, Dutch, and French representation.

In order to bring to the notice of these nations the necessity of the strict enforcement of their laws, the Quakers

[67] Meeting of the Committee of Friends, York, May 21, 1807.
[68] *Information respecting the present state of the Slave-Trade, with a Proposal for a subscription to aid in promoting the object of its total abolition.*

issued a proclamation to all the peoples of Europe, which was distributed, translated into the various languages, at the courts and in other influential places.[69] This proclamation constitutes renewed proof of the extraordinary energy and self-sacrifice of numerous members of the Society, whose strength was often applied to many widely different projects at the same time.

The next year (1823) the Society for the Gradual Abolition of Slavery in our Colonies was founded in London; and the establishment of branch societies throughout the length and breadth of the land was vigorously promoted by William Allen.[70] In Parliament, too, there now began a new phase of the movement.

Whereas Wilberforce, in the earlier years, had taken the term "emancipation" in the sense of a milder or more humane type of serfdom, he now accepted the position laid down in a new Quaker petition, and demanded the abolition of slavery in any and all forms.[71] The presentation of further proposals in accordance with this point of view was reserved for his successor, Sir Thomas Fowell Buxton, a Quaker by extraction and by temperament, though he did not officially belong to the Society at the time at which he came into prominence.[72]

[69] *Address to the Inhabitants of Europe on the Iniquity of the Slave-Trade: "Cries of Africa,"* 1822. French and Italian translations are still extant. The challenge to abolish slavery is prefaced by an exhaustive account of the methods of capturing and transporting the slaves.

[70] Sherman, *op. cit.,* p. 382.

[71] See Uhden, *op. cit.,* p. 368ff.

[72] Among his literary contributions to the movement, an exhaustive discussion of the slave trade deserves mention: *The African Slave-Trade and its Remedy,* London 1840. This treatise showed that during the twenty years since slave trading had been officially abolished, an average

Buxton's proposal to declare slavery to be irreconcilable with the Christian religion and with the British constitution did not pass; but the government addressed a letter to all colonial governments, recommending various reforms. The suggestions included lightening the tasks, limitation of the right of overseers to administer punishment, and granting the right to the Negroes to purchase their own freedom; but, as was to be expected, the planters objected to such restriction. The risings of the slaves that occurred from time to time were charged to the abolitionists, and for a while made their cause very unpopular, so that all progress was checked. But this applied only to Parliament: nothing could stop the friends of the Negroes in their forward march. In 1824 the Quakers again found it necessary to circulate pamphlets on the slave trade all over England and in Holland and France, citing passages from the *Sierra Leone Gazette* as authentic proof that the trade still existed;[73] and they distributed also a report on the above-mentioned colony of free Negroes.

In the course of the year 1824, there were established, with the coöperation of the Quakers, various other societies for the encouragement of trade with Africa and the substitution of products of free labor for articles made with slave labor in the colonies; the Society for the

---

of approximately 200,000 slaves annually had been taken from Africa, but that only 3% of the slave ships had been caught. The effect of the law, since smaller vessels were now being used, was only to make the conditions of transportation worse. A voyage was considered to have come out well when between 30% and 50% of the slaves reached their destination alive.

[73] In spite of the legal prohibition, the newspaper contained notices about buying and selling slaves.

Purpose of Encouraging the Black Settlers of Sierra Leone and the Natives of Africa Generally in the Cultivation of their Soil by the Sale of their Produce, and the Tropical-Free-Labour Company were among the number. In the production of indigo free labor was already able to compete with slave labor, and the plan of the societies was to attain the same goal for sugar and wool. For this purpose a company was formed with a capital of £4,000,-000, in shares of a par value of £5.

We have no further data as to the activity of this company, but we may assume that it had a successful development from the reports of the production of East Indian sugar, grown by free labor. The costs of production of this sugar were, it was claimed, below those of the sugar grown by the West Indian slaveholders; but as a result of higher import duties the East Indian sugar was more expensive than the West Indian. The hope was expressed, however, that a trifling difference in price should not be the deciding factor, when it was a matter of protecting human rights or even human lives.[74]

Another society, the Association for the Relief of Some Cases of Great Distress in the Island of Antigua among the Discarded Negroes, etc., appears to owe its existence exclusively to Quakers. Care was extended to those in need of assistance exactly as within the Quaker community; lists were maintained of the persons who were regularly supported, similar to those in the monthly meet-

[74] The following calculation, which is not exactly lucid, is appended to an advertisement of the East Indian sugar: "A family which consumes 5 pounds of sugar a week, can prevent the 'murder' of one of their fellow men by the use of East Indian sugar instead of West Indian over a period of 21 months; 8 such families, in 19½ years, can prevent the enslaving or murder of 100."

ings. The annual report of 1827 calls this association a strong helper in combating the piteous misery of freed Negroes.

These latter naturally needed counsel and education everywhere; but though organization on a large scale would have been desirable for this purpose, we hear only of modest beginnings. The services of Hannah Kilham in this connection should not be forgotten. This woman went alone to Africa, set up schools for the natives in Sierra Leone, and, with the approval of the governor, looked out for the interests of the freed children of slaves.[75] She also greatly desired to effect the instruction of the Africans in the intelligent cultivation of their land, so that periods of famine could be avoided—preferably through model farms to be worked in connection with the local schools. The Quaker committee on the abolition of slavery held the same view, but appears to have given only financial help to establishments founded by others. It contributed, for instance, toward the setting up of schools by Baptist preachers.[76] For other tasks appeared to them to be more urgent: it would be time enough to go at the problem of training and helping the freed slaves in accordance with a broad social policy of rehabilitation when their emancipation had actually been attained. And toward this goal, in spite of manifold efforts,[77] very little progress was made in the next twenty years.

But in 1831 a renewed and violent attack was made

[75] See *Memoir of Hannah Kilham, chiefly compiled from her journal and edited by her daughter-in-law,* Sarah Biller, London 1837, ch. 13.
[76] Yearly Meeting Minutes for 1826.
[77] See, for example, the Quaker petition of June 17, 1828.

upon Parliament: nearly 500 petitions supported Buxton's motion. Following the advice of Joseph Sturge, who had recognized that the demands as hitherto made were not practicable, the Quakers now urged immediate emancipation. When their address was delivered to Parliament, Buxton gave expression to his very great pleasure that this renewed pronouncement should come from the Society of Friends, which had been the first to declare that the buying, selling, and holding of slaves was irreconcilable with the Christian religion (1688), from which the first petition for the abolition of the slave trade had been received (1783), and by which the first petition for the complete abolition of slavery had also been presented (1823).[78] Now at last Parliament declared for abolition, but postponed the date at which the act should take effect until the reimbursal due the planters should be determined. Only the slaves belonging to the crown were immediately freed (March 12, 1818).

With this act the program of the abolitionists was approximately realized, and the greater part of the Antislavery Society adopted an attitude of awaiting developments. Only a small group, the so-called Agency Committee, under the leadership of Joseph Sturge and James Cropper, continued its activity, in order to continue to do propaganda work;[79] for the experience of 1807 showed that further agitation of the matter would very

[78] See *Memoirs of Sir Thomas Fowell Buxton, edited by his son,* Charles Buxton, London 1866, p. 269.

[79] It is astonishing to read what sacrifices the little Quaker community made, in spite of their many other charitable obligations, for the antislavery movement. In the years 1830-32 the sum of £3000 was given to the Antislavery Society alone (Reports of the Committee of 1830-31-32).

probably be required.[80] The Society also published a new essay on the subject of slavery,[81] which culminated in the demand for immediate abolition.

When conditions of emancipation were finally settled, the hopes which the abolitionists had cherished were still unfulfilled. The Act of August 28, 1833, effective August 1, 1834,[82] did, to be sure, declare that all Negroes were free; but, in spite of a sum appropriated for compensation of the planters amounting to £20,000,000, a seven-year period of service was required of the Negroes. This period was euphemistically called a term of apprenticeship, and was defended as a wisely provided preparation for freedom; but, as a matter of fact, it was utilized for unlimited exploitation.

The repeal of this clause of the act was now the object of the labors of the abolitionists. Protests against it, and petitions of the Quakers,[83] were supported by authentic reports from Friends, who, in the course of thorough investigations of conditions in the colonies, found their worst fears far surpassed. Under the eyes of the English officials there the existing laws against the slave trade and slaveholding were generally disregarded.[84] "One

[80] In this connection see also Richard, *Memoir of Joseph Sturge,* p. 203ff.

[81] *Some reflections on the subject of slavery, respectfully submitted on behalf of the Religious Society of Friends to the Christian Public in the British Dominions,* January 4, 1833.

[82] *An Act for the abolition of slavery, throughout all the British Colonies, for promoting the industry of the manumitted slaves, and for compensating the persons hitherto entitled to the services of such slaves.*

[83] For instance, the petition of 1835.

[84] The officials found themselves in the same boat with the planters: they usually owned slaves themselves. Of seventeen colonial officials in the Dominican Republic (then called Dominica), for instance, there were only two who were not slave owners (Letter from Dominica, March 1, 1835).

cannot imagine anything more terrible than compulsory labor under this law; unmitigated slavery was as nothing in comparison with present conditions," wrote Sturge. From 1837 on he instituted agitation on a large scale,[85] in order to inform the English as to the actual working of the Abolition Act, and to bring pressure to bear upon the government.

When the Friends of the Negroes, seeking relief in Parliament, were defeated there,[86] the colonies set out to help themselves, and on August 3, 1838, the seven-year term of service was abolished.[87] The Quakers at once instituted a system of assisting the freed slaves. Attempts of the former slaveowners to keep wages unreasonably low, or to drive off the Negroes from their homesteads, were met by the purchase of tracts of land upon which the freed slaves were placed in colonies. Thus even in the West Indies the Quaker principle was observed: When help is given, it should be thoroughgoing, and such as will enable the recipient ultimately to stand upon his own feet.[88]

After the Quakers had finally attained their goal in the English colonies, they turned, full of energy, to the support of the abolitionist movement in the United States,[89]

[85] Through the establishment of a Central Negro Emancipation Committee.

[86] The Quakers too had sent in a petition, in 1838, for the repeal of the apprenticeship clause.

[87] The chief reason probably was the fear that further agitation would lead to risings in the colonies. Emancipation had been attended by no disturbances: the whole process was carried out in very good order.

[88] See Richard, op. cit., p. 201.

[89] See H. von Holst, The Constitutional and Political History of the United States (translation from the German Verfassung und Demokratie der Vereinigten Staaten von Amerika), 8 vols., Chicago 1889-1892, i, 278: "The Quakers have the honor of having begun the agitation from this

where the work had to be begun at the beginning again. Only a few scattered Quakers there [90] had remained true to the cause, as the battle had been drawn out over the decades and the situation became worse and worse. The Society had officially withdrawn into private life, in order not to "endanger its own purity by the uncleanness of politics." For the striking growth of the cotton industry as a result of various inventions,[91] and the tremendously increased English demand,[92] appeared to many persons to justify the continuance and even the extension of slavery,[93] so that in spite of the legal prohibition, the importation of slaves continued on a very large scale.

Nevertheless, the English Friends finally succeeded in stirring the American meetings to action again,[94] and every attempt was made to induce England [95] and other

standpoint [i.e., the morality of slavery] earliest, and most radically." See also p. 307. The Quakers had begun their agitation as early as 1790 (see pp. 89, 93). In 1832 the New England Antislavery Society was founded; in 1833 there was held a national antislavery convention in Pennsylvania, the practical result of which was the establishment of the American Antislavery Society.

[90] Among these may be mentioned Benjamin Lundy, who founded the *Genius of Universal Emancipation,* the first published organ of the abolitionists in America, and as a traveling preacher agitated for immediate and unconditioned emancipation; and the poet John Greenleaf Whittier, who became famous for his songs of freedom.

[91] Principally as the result of Eli Whitney's cotton gin (1793), by means of which a single slave could separate the cotton seeds from about 1000 pounds of cotton a day, instead of five or six pounds, as formerly.

[92] The export of cotton in 1790 amounted to 189,000 pounds, in 1843 to over a billion pounds.

[93] In 1790 there were 679,000 slaves in the United States; in 1843 there were 2,847,810. See also Richard, *op. cit.,* p. 114.

[94] In 1839, Sturge founded the British and Foreign Antislavery Society, and tried to enlist all American Quakers under its banner.

[95] In 1849, the Society of Friends presented a memorial to Queen Victoria, in which she is asked to use her influence upon America.

European states [96] to use their friendly influence upon America; but the agitation remained as fruitless as the efforts to enable cotton that was the product of free labor to compete in production costs with slave-made cotton. Concrete benefits accrued only to the labors of those committees of Quakers in Philadelphia, New York, and other cities of the northern half of the Union, which later, during the Civil War, took care of fugitive slaves from the South.[97] Note should also be made of the organization, as a result of Quaker efforts, of a great English association for assisting emancipated slaves (the Freedmen's Aid Society), which gave the American associations valuable material aid, when, after the end of the Civil War, the final abolition of slavery caused a great increase in the number of destitute blacks.

The efforts of the Quakers in behalf of the Negroes are carried on into the present time, for as yet their goal, the eradication of slavery throughout the world, has not been attained. The Antislavery Committee of the Meeting for Sufferings of the London Yearly Meeting is constantly engaged in making investigations and presenting its findings to officials in authority; Friends deserve much of the credit for the freeing of the Negroes in Zanzibar and Pemba in 1909. In their far-flung missionary settlements both men and women, so far as strength permits, interest themselves in the emancipated slaves; the task of assisting the long oppressed race is counted a privilege, which the Society has inherited from past generations.[98]

[96] After 1850 the same memorial was sent to all the courts of Europe by William Edward Forster.

[97] See the Reports of the Meeting for Sufferings on the subscriptions in aid of colored refugees from 1862 on.

[98] See the Yearly Meeting Minutes for 1910.

CHAPTER SEVEN

CONCLUSION

ALL the humanitarian work of the Quakers, as we have followed it in various fields, is based upon their conception of the close interdependence of the individual members of the social group; for they assume the validity of this conception in its broadest sense, extending its application beyond the church congregation to include the nation and ultimately humanity itself. Moreover, they regard each human soul as having a more than merely personal worth; and this view leads them to a position quite antagonistic to those whose philosophy of life is on a lower economic, intellectual, and even moral plane. From this attitude are derived demands which they make upon the more fortunate to share their good fortune; for the Quakers do not acknowledge the right of the wealthy to make their wealth of service only to themselves. And with this conception the medieval view of the poor and needy as necessary in order that the upper classes may have an object for their charity, falls to the ground. The practices of the so-called "mercantile state" are also rejected, which considered hunger and poverty useful as incentives to work, and, by establishing maximum wage rates, interfered with the natural development of the laboring classes into economic security, and confirmed the privileged classes in their more favored situation.

CONCLUSION

A living wage is not only no longer feared, but on the contrary demanded as a human right. Liberal help is extended to the poor with the purpose of eliminating as much as possible the *causes* of their poverty. This purpose explains the strict individualization of their care and their encouragement to self-help, which they believe is reënforced by spiritual and moral uplift.

By efforts such as these the Quakers in England laid the foundations for modern social work long before the abortive character of public poor relief as actually practiced had been recognized at all. Even Malthus pointed out specifically that the methods of relief then current in England tended toward the permanent increase of poverty. In the controversy that his writings brought on, there were occasional references to the conditions that existed within the Quaker community, where liberal care of the poor was accompanied by very slight increase in their number; [1] but people did not see that the granting of a wage sufficient for a decent living is the strongest incentive to steady work—an incentive of a kind which never enters the mind of the hopeless pauper.

Whoever wishes to influence the entire life of the worker has no need to fear any unfavorable effects of higher wages nor of the elevation of broad masses of humanity out of sodden ignorance. The dangers of one-sided education are met in Quaker communities through the religious basis of all instruction and the close feeling

[1] See, for instance, John Barton, *An Inquiry into the Causes of the Progressive Depreciation of Agricultural Labour in Modern Times,* London 1820. He claims that the ratio of births to deaths among the Quakers was 22:21, as compared with 28:19 in the average of all England.

of fraternity with those who belong to other classes of society, resulting in mutual understanding and respect. This result is helped along by the esteem in which professional or skilled labor is held in all circles, by the conscious giving up of luxuries and many external pleasures, and by the love for a comfortable home, intimate family life, and instructive reading.

For it is characteristic of the Quakers that they disapprove of reading, in their leisure hours, the ordinary type of moralizing and strongly sectarian propagandist literature, and prefer to occupy themselves with nature study and history. The habit of enjoying this type of mental recreation was also effective, like the training in spiritual insight, in the fight against alcohol. This fight was further helped by the practice of total abstinence by their members, who, though substantially enough established to be able to drink spirituous liquors without suffering any serious economic harm, yet gave an example of restraint to the day laborers who could not afford such indulgence. For only one who acts in every respect as he asks others to act is qualified to lead the sinner back to grace.

The building up of a considerable number of morally lofty personalities within the confines of the Quaker communities may perhaps justify their exclusiveness,[2] and the strict policy of the earlier generations (which can hardly be reconciled with their steady emphasis upon toleration) with regard to the expulsion of erring members—the more so as there is no evidence of any lenience toward

[2] The desire was to maintain the Society upon a high ethical plane, in order that there might be a group, however small, in which the principles of Quakerism should be preserved serenely safe against all attacks.

CONCLUSION

moral backsliders. Nowadays expulsions are quite rare:
six in 1890, 7 in 1900, four in 1910.

The Quakers stop at nothing when the saving of a human soul is at stake. So, for example, they have been
fighting for decades against the "state regulation of vice,
the crowning crime of Christendom." [3] They stand for
the protection of woman—even of the fallen woman, who
prejudices the law in favor of men, and at the same time
injures the reputation of many innocent women.

Their goal, the winning and holding of useful members
of the social and religious group, is pursued even among
those who suffer under mental disease. The Quakers
deserve the credit for awakening England to a more
humane attitude toward this peculiarly unfortunate
affliction, which previously had seemed to rob its
victims of all claims upon the public for humane treatment.

It was the ultimate utilization, by the nation as a whole,
of the experience which the Quakers gained in the limited confines of their own communities that lent to the
social work of the Quakers its first real significance.
Though it is true, of course, that their experience in some
lines of work was less easily applied than in others, nevertheless many of their fundamental ideas deserve the wid-
est possible acceptance. The Friends themselves have
done effective work in making their ideas known through
their public protests against social evils and their peti-

---

[3] The Friends' Association for Abolishing the State Regulation of Vice,
though not the first organization of its kind (the London Rescue Society
preceded it), has labored unremittingly for the repeal of the Contagious
Diseases (of Women) Acts of 1864, 1866, and 1869. See also the pamphlet *The Crowning Crime of Christendom,* by M. Gregory, London 1896.

tions for redress, and they have also apparently influenced other private organizations, whose social activities have much in common with their own.[4]

The frequent coöperation of the Quakers with others tends to obscure the evidence of their originality; and they have often taken ideas already extant and brought them to realization. This may be seen from the fact that they were always anxious to learn from foreign countries.[5] Moreover, their own activity is hard to gauge in its full extent, since they have never sought recognition in their humanitarian labors, but remained modestly behind the cause for which they labored, and were content with the most thankless tasks.

Work in behalf of the less favored is for them a duty gladly fulfilled; even men whose days are much occupied with professional work use whatever small amount of free time they have in the service of the community. For, though the ascetic trait of Puritanism is beginning to weaken among modern Quakers, and a keen enjoyment of art is no more regarded as a forbidden pastime, they nevertheless feel that it is not right to indulge themselves too often in emotions of this type so long as there is such an infinite amount of serious work for them to do. What a contrast to the estheticism of the upper classes, now extending more and more widely, is afforded by this deep-

[4] Thus, for instance, the Society for Promoting Christian Knowledge, established in 1698, founded schools for the poor, and labored for moral reform; and later the Methodists, consciously or unconsciously, adopted many of the social ideas of the Quakers.

[5] Even in the earlier days of Quakerism, Bellers was well informed regarding the social institutions of other countries. The later Quakers on their numerous journeys always tried to gain an insight into relief work.

rooted conviction of the obligations of each individual toward his fellow men!

Thus the Quakers seem in these latter days to be called, as it were, for the strengthening of the world's sense of social responsibility. As yet we are hardly even standing on the threshold of what could be accomplished if each one would recognize and perform his duty. The Quakers of to-day consider that one of the chief needs of society is an improvement in the conditions under which great masses of mankind perform their daily labor. They do not demand a leveling off of all class differences, but a mitigation of the feverish intensity of business competition, in which the worker is too often sacrificed to the greed of the capitalists for profits. If, when investing money in an enterprise, the investor would take into consideration not only the return to be secured, but the working conditions of the employees, if every consumer would take the trouble to seek out those goods which brought a living wage to the workers who manufactured them, and did not injure their health—under these conditions, the Quakers believe, production would gradually turn in the desired direction.[6]

Even one who adopts a skeptical attitude with regard to the possibility of realizing this ideal, must join with the Quakers in affirming the necessity of stirring wider and wider circles to an interest in social problems.[7] A more penetrating understanding of such questions may

[6] See *The Stewardship of Wealth,* message from the Yearly Meeting of 1910.

[7] An organization called the Friends' Social Union has been serving this purpose for a number of years. It attempts to stimulate an active interest in social questions among Quakers and in the Adult Schools, and to make the members useful in practical social work.

lead to an increased measure of self-sacrifice, and make way more and more for the Quaker precept that wealth and ability are like talents which are entrusted to man to be faithfully administered and properly used.

BIBLIOGRAPHICAL INDEX

The figures are page numbers of the present work on which the given entry is referred to. Figures in boldface designate the page on which the fullest bibliographical information is given.

BIBLIOGRAPHICAL INDEX

BIBLIOGRAPHICAL INDEX

BIBLIOGRAPHICAL INDEX

BIBLIOGRAPHICAL INDEX

BIBLIOGRAPHICAL INDEX

BIBLIOGRAPHICAL INDEX

GENERAL INDEX

An asterisk preceding a number indicates a reference in a footnote; an asterisk in parentheses following a number indicates a reference both in the text and in a footnote.

A

GENERAL INDEX

GENERAL INDEX

Birth rate, *235
Blackbourne, (or Blackbury), Sara, 67
"Black Guard," 169
Board schools, 118(*)
Book of Sports, 38
Bootham, school at, *116
Boston, Mass., 140
Bournville, 98*, 142
Box Meeting, 68(*)
  Assumed care of needy, 68
Boycott of slave-made articles, 221
Boys, instructed at Ackworth in three
  R's, gardening, and domestic chores,
  114
  School for, at Bootham, *116
Bradford, 97
Braithwaite, William Charles, *163
Brandenburg, *57
Brandy and wine imported from France,
  133
Bread distributed after business meet-
  ings, 64, 65(*)
Breda, Declaration of, 38
Bridewell, public floggings at, 168
Bright, John, 97
  Student at Ackworth, 116
Brighton, District Visiting Society in,
  95
Bristol, 12, 35, 86(*), 112, *154, 216
Bristol and Somerset Quarterly Meet-
  ing, *86
British and Foreign Antislavery Society,
  *232
British and Foreign School Society, 125,
  126
British and Foreign School Society, *120
British and Foreign Temperance Society,
  140
Brookfield Agricultural School, 108
Browne, Robert, leader of Independents,
  21
"Bubbles" (speculative enterprises), *89
Burial of destitute persons, 64
Burials, Quakers use no priest at, 28
Burlington, New Jersey, *207
Burning at stake, penalty for noncon-
  formity, 20
Burroughs, Edward, 42
Business, feverish pursuit of, con-
  demned, 239
Buxton, Anna, 186
Buxton, Thomas Fowell, *175, 186(*),
  187, 188(*), *189
  Labors for prison reform, 179
  Visits prisons with E. Fry, 186
  Visits prisons throughout Europe, 194
  Succeeds W. Wilberforce as advocate
    of abolition of slavery in Parlia-
    ment, 225
  Presents motion in 1831 for immediate
    abolition of slavery, 229

C

Cadbury, George, 98, 142
Calvin, John, 31
Canons and Institutions of G. Fox, 42
Capital punishment of insane, 152
  Imposed for 150 different crimes, 166
  Indirectly abolished in 1653, 167
  Crimes punished by, reduced, 193(*)
  Abolition of—
    Except for murder, urged by G.
      Fox, 167, 169
    Complete, J. Bellers urges, 169
    Credit for priority in urging, be-
      longs to J. Bellers, *170
    Quakers labor for, 191
Capitalists among Quakers, 87
Carlyle, Thomas, 97(*)
Carolina, constitution for, framed by J.
  Locke, *200
Case work in giving help to the poor,
  63, 69, 72
Catholics, Roman, leniency of, toward
  human frailty, 30
  Clergy of, objects of G. Fox's attacks,
    30
  T. Waldmeier left, to become Quaker,
    160
Central Negro Emancipation Committee,
  *231
Chancery, Court of, notorious, 167
Charity as exercised by church inter-
  fered with by Reformation, 144
  Motivated by hope of salvation, 144(*)
Charity organization urged in place of
  unregulated almsgiving, 56
Charity schools, 120
Charles I, *51
Charles II, *67
  Returns to throne in 1660, 37
  Issues Declaration of Breda, *38
  Deeds tract in America to W. Penn,
    46
  Protests at wasting time in alehouses,
    133
  Repeals some, confirms others, of
    Cromwell's enactments, 167(*)
Chartist movement, 97
Chelsea, 185
Chester, Penna., *206
Child labor brought on by poverty, 55
Children conduct Quaker meetings, 39
  Instructed in elementary subjects at
    Clerkenwell, 84, 85
  Specially cared for in New Lanark, 96
  Help defray expense of own education,
    105
  Education of, important to Penn, 110
  Employment of, in gainful occupa-
    tions, unsatisfactory, 112
  Set to work at Ackworth, 113

251

GENERAL INDEX

Children should be "hardly bred," says
W. Penn, 115
  Duty of providing with education, 117
  Quakers would not exploit, 117
  Rich and poor educated alike, 117
  In cloth factories at four years of age,
  *117
  Of Quakers, many now educated in
  public schools, 119
  In England and Wales estimated at
  2,000,000 in 1800, 121
  Educated cheaply or free in Lancaster
  schools, 124
  Sunday Schools organized for, 126
  Influence of mothers upon, 128
  To be accustomed to moderation in
  use of spirituous liquors, 134
  In Newgate prison, 177, 179
  Homeless, in London, 169(*), 186
"Children of the Light," 30
  Quakers at first called themselves 80,
  34
Christianity, primitive, considered same
  as Quakerism, 30
Christus mysticus, 24
Chronicles of Newgate, *182
Circulating schools, 127
Civil War (of England), 50, 55, 166
Civil War (of the U. S.), 233
Clarkson, Thomas, 197(*), 208, 216(*),
  218(*)
  Dedicated to antislavery work, 214
  Prize essay of, on slavery, 214(*)
Clergy, Quakers reject, as a separate
  group, 25
Clerkenwell workhouse, established in
  1702, 82
  Charges at, 83, 112
  Used by persons not entirely destitute,
  83
  Instruction of children in, 84, 85
  Deficits in operation of, 84
  Ceases to exist as such in 1811, 84
  Becomes school, 85
  Reasons for abandonment of, 85, 86
  Idea of, revived in monthly meeting
  schools, 106
  Becomes high-grade school for middle
  and upper classes, 116
  Exists now as Saffron Walden School,
  116
  Allows "sufficient beer" in the rations,
  131
Coal, high price of, 63, 64(*)
  Given to needy, 63, 64
Coeducation, 103, *116
  Universal in Pennsylvania, 110(*)
Coinage, debasement of, by Henry VIII,
  51
College of industry, proposed by J.
  Bellers, **76**

College of industry, idea of, urged in
  epistle on education, 105
Colonies of freedmen set up, 231
Colonies at Home of W. Allen, 92
*Committee of Manners, Education, and
  Arts,* *110
*Committee for promoting the Royal Lan-
  castrian System for the Education of
  the Poor,* *124
Common-field system of agriculture,
  51(*)
Competition considered harmful by J.
  Bellers, 79
Concentration of population in cities,
  92
Condorcet, Marquis de, *218
Confiscation of property of Quakers, 104
Conformity, declaration of, required of
  officials, 37
Conservative group of Quakers in Eng-
  land, *48
Consumers' coöperation, *97
Contagious Diseases (of women) Acts,
  *237
Conventicle Act, 45
Conventional forms of politeness, dis-
  pensed with by Quakers, 29
Convict labor, 181
Convicts, see **Prisoners**
Corporation Act of 1661, 37
  Repealed, 48
Cost of living raised by monopolies in
  16th and 17th centuries, 51
  Above income of average laborer, 52
  Dropped in 18th century, 86
Cotton industry, extension of, appeared
  to justify slavery in the U. S., 232
Court of Justice, European, proposed by
  G. Fox, 28
Craftsmen, skilled, migrate from France
  to England, *55
Crimean War, 152
Cromwell, Henry, 36
Cromwell, Oliver, 50, *57, 132(*), 167,
  200
  Included among the Independents, *21
  Quakers in his army, 35
  His severity toward blasphemers, 35
  Petition to, *36
  G. Fox opposes his taking the crown,
  36
  Personal interview with Fox, 37(*)
  Death, 37
  Recognized need of reform in penal
  code, 166, 167
Cromwell, Richard, 37
Crook, John, 42
Cropper, James, 229
Cultivation of soil natural occupation,
  92
Cumberland, 60

252

GENERAL INDEX

D

Dale, David, founder of New Lanark colony, 96
Dancing not taught to Quaker children, 101
Danish, learning of, recommended, 112
Darlington, 139
Deaconesses, 150
Deaf-mutes, 158(*)
Debasement of coinage by Henry VIII, 51
Debt, imprisonment for, *172
Debtors, relief afforded to, 167
Confined with insane and other prisoners, 178
Declaration of Breda, 38
Defoe, Daniel, laments unusued land, *92
Delaware River, early Quaker settlement on, 45
Deportation, 170
Of women, to New South Wales, *183
Of undesirables, under Cromwell, *200
Of vagabonds, noncomformists, etc., *201
Desertion by man of the family frequent, *62
Devonshire, Quakers in, advise against handing strong liquors to others, 137
Devonshire House, 5, 7, 106, *107
Diet of middle classes in 17th century, *133
For the sick, 144
Discipline, 47, *140
Duty of monthly meeting to maintain, 61
Disorderly conduct a cause of disownment, 134
Disownment, for drunkenness, 134
Summary of cases of, 134(*)
Dissection of dead bodies urged by J. Bellers, 145
Division of labor, 55
Doles, 92(*), 95
Dominica (Dominican Republic), *230
Dowry funds, 71
Dreyfus case, compared with trial of W. Penn and W. Meade, *45
Drinking a cause of disownment, 134
See also **Spirituous liquors**
Dublin (Bucks County, Penn.), 203
Duel, opposition of A. Benezet to, *206
Durham, 60, *61
Dutch, learning of, recommended, 112

E

Eastern Penitentiary in Pennsylvania, *188
Eaton, Joseph, 141
Economist, 116

Eden, Sir Frederick Morton, 12, *126
Edict of Nantes, *55
Edinburgh Quarterly Meeting, 108
Edmundson, William, *103, *198
Education, 99
A special concern of Quakers, 79(*)
In Bellers's College of Industry, 79, 80
"Beyond reading and writing, not so useful as some think" (J. Bellers), 80
Need of masses for, first agitated by Puritans, 99
Free compulsory, urged by J. Harrington, 99
In public schools, unacceptable to Quakers, 100
Assistance for, given without publicity, 100
Annual reports on, *100
No general Quaker theory on till 1850, 101
Emphasis on religious instruction, 101
To include "whatsoever things were civil and useful in creation," 101
To be practical as well as spiritual, 102
Higher, not required for ministers, 102
Constant concern of Yearly Meeting, 104
Should enable recipient to earn a living, 105
Industrial slant of theories regarding, 106
Among English Quakers in the 18th century, 111
Expense of, in London, 112
Objections to, answered, 112, 113(*)
Duty to provide children with, 117
Required in order to make population productive of wealth (J. Bellers), 148
Compulsory in Pennsylvania, 173
Lack of, begets criminality, 185
Of slaves, urged by G. Fox, 198
Of Negro children in America, 221
Of lower classes, not to be feared, 235
Education Bill of 1870 the outcome of Quaker activity, *119
Education, popular, advanced by Quakers, 120
Advocated by A. Smith and Malthus, 120
The government indifferent to, 120
Not to be feared, 121
Educational statistics for 1909, 119
Elders, duties of, 40, 62, 63, 103
Elizabeth, Queen of England, *19, 29, *51, 52(*), 53, 199
Elizabeth Fry Refuge, 195(*)
Ellwood, Thomas, 82, 105
Emigration discouraged unless likely to be advantageous, 69

253

GENERAL INDEX

GENERAL INDEX

Fox, George, accounts of miraculous cures, 145(*)
Opposed capital punishment except for murder, 167, 169
Attitude toward slavery, 197, 198
Missionary journey to Barbados and Jamaica, *198
Urged missionary teachers to give Negroes Christian instruction, 199
Fox, Joseph, 96
Fox, Samuel, in Adult School movement, 127
Frame of Government of Penna., *110, 172
France, 44, *55
Quaker missionary activity in, 43
Antislavery propaganda in, 226
Frankfort, English fugitives in, 19
German colonists from, 202
Franklin, Benjamin, *109
Freedmen, colonies of, set up, 231
Quakers care for—
In colonial America, 215
In Africa, 228
In British colonies, 231
In U. S. during Civil War, 233
Freedmen's Aid Society, 233
Free Society of Traders, 135, 202
Free trade advanced by Quakers, 96, 97
French, learning of, recommended, 112
Friends, Society of: Quakers officially so designated, 34
See **Quakers; Quakerism**
Friends' Association for Abolishing the State Regulation of Vice, *237
Friends' Educational Society, 117
Friends' First Day School Association, *130
Friends of the Negroes, *218
Friends' Social Union, *239
"Friends of Thieves," 185
"Friends of Truth," early name of Quakers, 34
Friends' Temperance Union, 141
Frivolity of the upper classes, 37
Fry, Elizabeth (Gurney), 84, 177, 186(*), 190
Bibliography on, *95, *178
Aids poor relief in Brighton, 95
Works for nurses' training school, 151(*)
Consults with T. Fliedner, 151, 194(*)
Organizes prison reform in Newgate, 177
Converted by W. Savery, *177
Gives clothes to women prisoners, 177
Brilliant success of, 182(*)
Visits departing convict ships, 184
Establishes school for homeless girls, 185

Fry, Elizabeth (Gurney), secures appointment of matrons and prison overseers, 193
Before commissions of House of Commons, 193, 194
Visited prisons throughout Europe, 194
Elizabeth Fry Refuge named for, 195(*)
Funds for helping apprentices, 106
For higher education, 118
For assisting young people to set up in business, 118
Placed at J. Lancaster's disposal, 124

G

Gaming a cause of disownment, 134
Garden city at Bournville, 98(*)
General Meeting at London, *106
At York, *157
Genius of Universal Emancipation, *232
Gentleman's Magazine, *149
George I, 208
George II, *86
George III, *113, *125, *157, 211
Germans in distress helped by Quakers, *90
Germantown, 110, 202, 203(*)
Germany, spread of Quakerism in, 60
Gilbert's Act, 91(*)
Girls, at Ackworth taught needlework and housekeeping, 114
School for, at The Mount, *116
Homeless, in London, 184
Gloucester, Duke of, 223
Goodridge, James, 137
Goodson, Dr., offers to erect house for insane, 154
Greenwood, John, *21
Grellet, Stephen, interested E. Fry in prisons, 177(*), 186
Griffith, John, *88
Protests against slavery, *207
Grubb, Edward, *119
Grubb, Sarah, *115
Guilds, decline of, 52(*)
Gurney, Elizabeth, *177. See **Fry**, Elizabeth (Gurney)
Gurney, Joseph John, improves religious instruction at Ackworth, 114
Visits prisons with his sister, E. Fry, 186
Urges others to visit prisons, *190
Visits foreign prisons, 194
Gurney, Samuel, 151, 186, 194
Guy's Hospital, London, 150

H

Hales, John, *51
Hard labor as punishment not favored, 189

255

GENERAL INDEX

GENERAL INDEX

GENERAL INDEX

GENERAL INDEX

GENERAL INDEX

Nursing becomes a profession for educated women, 151

Nursing association(s) in Germany, 150
First, set up in England, 151

O

Oaths, Quakers do not take or administer, 28

Oceana of J. Harrington describes ideal state, 99(*)

Old Bailey, 45

One-price system, origin of, credited to Quaker merchants, 11, *87

Organization plan of the Society of Friends, 59

Organization of laborers forbidden by law, 55

Ormonde, Duke of, 44

Orphans received at Clerkenwell, *85
Homeless, duty of society to, 169(*)

Orthodox Friends, *47

Overseers, duties of, 40, 62, 63

Owen, Robert, 82
Takes over management of New Lanark, 96
Conflict with Quakers, *96
Helped J. Lancaster, *125

P

Palatinate, 202(*)

Palestine, Quaker missionary activity in, 43
Insane asylum in, 160

Parchappe, J. B. M., Inspector General in charge of the insane in France, *158

Paris, *152, *218

Parish poor fund, contributed to by Quakers, 66

Pastorius, Francis Daniel, 110(*)
Leader of emigrants from Palatinate to Pennsylvania, **202**(*)
Bee Hive, *202
Voices first public protest against slavery, 203

Patriotism, Quakers reproached with lack of, *28

Paul, Vincent de, 150

Pauperism, prevention of, 90

Paupers, number of, *67

Peel, Sir Robert, opposes municipalization of School of Discipline, 185

Pemba, freeing of Negroes in, 233

Pemberton, James, 209

Penal code, need of reform in, 166
In Pennsylvania, 172, 173
Quaker theory of reform of, 186, 191

Penington, Isaac, 113

Penitentiary for the Eastern District of Penna., *188

Penketh, school at, *116

Penn, William, 24, *27, 44, *62, 117, 138, 139(*), 168
Bibliography on, *43
Worked out plan of European court of justice, 28
Second founder of Quakerism, 43
Did not like court life, 44
Influenced by T. Loe, 44
Sent to France and Ireland, 44
Repeatedly imprisoned, 44
Disowned by his father, 44
Tried with W. Meade in Old Bailey, 45
Assists Quakers, 45
Establishes colony in Pennsylvania, 45
Purchases land from natives, 46
Returns to England, 46
Disapproves of extravagance, *58
Provides for partial employment bureau in Pennsylvania, *74
Friend of J. Bellers, *75
Circulates Bellers's epistle on education, 105
His views on education coincide with G. Fox's, 109
Educates his children carefully, 109(*)
Provides for education of children in Pennsylvania, 109, 110(*)
Had liberal education, 113
Educational principles adopted at Ackworth, 115
Stipulates that there shall be no alehouses in Pennsylvania, 134, 135
Regulations regarding prisons, 172
Does not abolish slavery in Pennsylvania, though troubled by it, 202
Holds slaves in Pennsylvania, 202
Induces Germans to emigrate to Pennsylvania, 202
In advance of his fellow believers regarding slavery, 205
Returns to England, 205

Penn, William (Admiral Penn), 44, 45, *46

Pennsylvania deeded to W. Penn, 46
Educational work of Quakers in, not representative of Penn's views, 108, 109
Settlers in, generally not cultivated persons, 109
University of, not essentially due to Quaker effort, *109
Behind England in advanced education, 109
Elementary education in, excellent, 109
Offered freer field than England for experimenting in temperance, 134

GENERAL INDEX

GENERAL INDEX

Prison reform, 162
Bibliography on, *186
Not engaged in by Quakers as official activity of the Society, but by individuals, 162
Need of, realized by Quakers from personal experience, 163
Quakers of early 18th century unresponsive to, 171
Makes progress in Pennsylvania, 172
Coöperation of officials for, necessary but lacking, 174
Attainable only as a result of pressure of public opinion, 174
Laws embodying Howard's proposals for, 175
In early 19th century, begins with E. Fry's work in Newgate, 178
Extends beyond Newgate, 182
Includes care of discharged prisoners, 183
Quaker theory on, clarified by experience, 186(*), 187

Prisons, conditions of, in England, 164, 174, 179
In Pennsylvania, 172, 173
Visited by the "Friends of Thieves," 185
Sanitary conditions in, 187(*)
Discipline, work, and training in, advocated, 189
Choice of jailers and matrons for, 190

Private schools set up by Friends or teachers acceptable to Friends, 103, 104
Establishment of, encouraged, 112

Prostitutes, a load of 100, sent to Virginia, *200
Sent to Sierra Leone, *220
Quakers protect, 237

Prostitution, 195
State regulation of, 237(*)

Provincial Schools of Friends, 108

Pryor, Elizabeth, 186

Public health, 143

Publicity of discussion of cases of those needing help, 62

Punishment secondary to reform, 188

Punishments for blasphemy, 35

Puritanism, origin in reign of Bloody Mary, 19
Reaction against, seen in repeal of Cromwell's reform laws, 167(*)
Among Quakers, diminishing, 238

Puritans, 167
First agitated need of education among the masses, 99
Founded Harvard University, *109
Persecution of, encouraged brutality and frivolity, 168

Q

Quaker: the name (="trembler") explained, 34

Quaker employers, 142

Quakerism granted freedom to develop under dominance of Saints, 21
Spread of, attended by troubles, 32
Disagreements within, in America, 47
Three groups within, in England, 48

Quaker movement, brief outline of, 19
Bibliography on, *19
Stimulated by persecution, 39
A second period begins with Restoration, 39
High tide at time of G. Fox's death, 47
In America, 43

Quaker railroad, 141

Quakers, bibliography of, *19
In industry, *9, 94
Prosperity follows persecution of, 10
Receive epithet "sly," 11
Leaders in humanitarian movements, 11
Withdraw from politics in Penna., 13
Outline history of, 19
Origin in 17th century, 19
Attitude toward Bible, 26
Ministry among, 26
Have no fixed confession of faith, 27
Do not use sacraments, 27
Do not take or administer oaths, 28
Do not bear arms, 28
Reproached with lack of patriotism, *28
Dispense with some conventional forms of politeness, 29
Urge avoidance of worldly diversions, 31
In Cromwell's army, 35
More than 3,000 imprisoned for disturbing the peace, 1656-58, *36
Called Nonconformists, 38
12,000 imprisoned under the later Stuarts, 39
1,200 prisoners released by Charles II, *45
Persecuted under Charles II, *45
Not tolerated in American colonies (except Rhode Island), *45
Withdraw from politics in Penna., 47
Number 70,000-80,000 in England at time of Fox's death, 47
Activity in poor relief, 50
100,000 members (in 1910) in America, *48
1,000 members (in 1910) in other lands, *48
Now attempt to avoid further separation, 48
19,000 members (in 1910) in England and Wales, 48

GENERAL INDEX

GENERAL INDEX

GENERAL INDEX

Sheffield, 140

Shillitoe, Thomas, **138**, 172, 176, 194
  Labors for prison reform, abolition of slavery, temperance, 138
  No trained group of helpers to carry on his reforms, 177

Sibforth, school at, *116

Sick, care of, 64

Sidcot, school at, *116

Sierra Leone, Negroes transported to, *220
  H. Kilham sets up schools in, 228(*)

Sierra Leone Company, 220

Sierra Leone Gazette, 226

Sieveking, Amalie, work of, in nursing associations, 151

Silk, winding, taught to children in Clerkenwell, 84

Silk industry, crisis in, 94
  Of London, centered in Spitalfields, 94

Simplicity urged as a duty of rich, 88

Singleton, William, pioneer in Adult School movement, 127

Sisters of charity, 150

Six Weeks' Meeting, 66, 153, *154
  Instructed to establish a school, 101

Skipton, 60

Slavery, Quaker, work against, **197**
  Considered compatible with the notion of the natural freedom of man, *200
  Considered analogous to case of redemptioners, 201
  In British colonies, contrasted with slavery in Spanish and Portuguese colonies, 201
  Existed in northern colonies of America less than in southern, 201
  Pastorius's protest against, 203
  Religious and moral arguments against, 203
  Practical arguments against, 203
  Question of, raised by Pastorius, but evaded by Monthly, Quarterly, and Yearly Meeting, 204(*)
  Considered to cause breakdown of religious life, 207(*)
  Decrease in, following London Yearly Meeting's decisive step, 208
  First attempt of Quakers to change British law regarding, 210(*)
  Indifference regarding, in England, 210
  Petition regarding, in House of Commons, 210, 211(*)
  Arguments against, recapitulated, 211, 212
  Arguments in support of, 219(*)
  In British colonies, attempt to regulate, resented, 226
  Renewed attack upon in 1831, 228
  Strengthened in the U. S. by the cotton industry, 232(*)

Slavery not yet eradicated, **233**
  Abolition of—
    Radical measures for, proposed by Quakers, 213
    Among the Quakers themselves, 215(*)
    Agitated anew in Parliament, 215
    Complete, agitation for, **223**
    Finally enacted by Parliament, to take effect 7 years later, 229
    Act for, 230(*)
    In British colonies, 231
  See also **Slaves; Slave trade; Negroes**

Slaves, first, in North American colonies, 200
  In British colonies, driven with severity, 201
  Provision in Penna. for freeing, after 14 years of service, 202
  Kept by W. Penn, 202
  Importation of, into Penna., discouraged by Quakers, 204
  Religious instruction of, urged by Quakers, 204, 205
  Tariff on importation of, into Penna., vetoed by the British crown, 205, 206
  Importation of, into Penna., prohibited, 205
  In southern colonies, could only be set free under certain conditions, 208(*)
  Emancipation of, urged by British Quakers, 211
  Export of, from U. S., prohibited in 1794, 221
  Even when freed by Abolition Act, required to work 7 years more for their owners, 230
  Imported into U. S. in spite of prohibition, 232
  Fugitive, assisted by Quakers during Civil War, 233
  Emancipated: see **Freedmen**

Slave ships, 216
  Overcrowding on, *219
  Became smaller after prohibition of slave trading, *226

Slave trade, Quaker work for abolition of, **197**
  Regulated in Assiento Treaty, 206(*)
  Discouraged by Chester Meeting, *206
  Protest against, by B. Lay, *207
  Legality of Parliamentary control of, debated, 217
  Abolition of, given precedence over abolition of slavery, 217
  Attempted regulation of, failed, 217
  Regulations of, made more exacting, 222
  Finally abolished by law on British ships, 222(*)

265

GENERAL INDEX

GENERAL INDEX

GENERAL INDEX

Visits of managing committee at Clerkenwell, 84

Voting not employed in Quaker business meetings, 41

W

Wage, living, 239
  Considered a human right, 235
  An incentive to work, 235
Wages depressed in 16th and 17th centuries, 52
  Fixed annually, 52(*)
  Lower in the north than in the south, *52
  Stationary as prices rose, 55, 56
  Rise in 18th century, 86
  Depressed by system of doles, 92
  Eked out by doles, *92
  Paid to apprentices during apprenticeship, 107
  Maximum, 234
  High, not to be feared, 235
Waldmeier, Theophilus, 160(*)
Wales, spread of Quakerism in, 60
  Circulating schools in, 127
Walker, John, 96
Waltham school for boys, 101
War of the Spanish Succession, 205
War Victims' Fund, *90
Wealth, considered by Wesley the result of religious revival and the cause of its decadence, 11
  Leads to luxury, 88
  Warning of dangers of, 89(*)
  Not considered strictly a personal possession, 234
  Stewardship of, *239, 240
Weather reports, first, published by Dr. John Fothergill, *149
Weaving, occupation of poor Friends at Bristol, 86
Wellington, Duke of, *192
Wesley, John, 11
West Indies, 198(*), *201, 231
Westminster, 183
Whitehead, George, *103
  Admonishes alehouse keepers, 136(*)
Whitney's cotton gin, *232
Whittier, John Greenleaf, *232
Wigton, school at, *116
Wilberforce, William, 214, 220
  Quaker efforts to secure reëlection of, 223
  Changes objective from "emancipation," or humane serfdom, to total abolition of slavery, 225
Wilburite Friends, *47
William Penn Charter School, 110
Wilson, James, 116

Wine and beer considered harmless by early Quakers, 131
  And brandy imported from France, 133
Women called as preachers as well as men, 25, 42(*)
  Equality with men, 42
  Character of, influenced by status among Quakers, 42
  Compelled to labor by prevalence of poverty, 55
  Organized by G. Fox to help sick and needy, 67
  Joined with Box Meeting, 68(*)
  Visited the poor in Clerkenwell, 84
  Theory of equality with men not observed at Ackworth, 114
  Committees of, in Friends' Educational Society, 117
  Included with men in Adult Schools, 128
  First Adult School classes formed for, 128
  Influence of, in home circle, 128
  No organized groups of, to do charitable work, 150
  Used for social work in Latin countries, 150
  Carried burden of keeping insane patients interested or amused, 157
  In Newgate prison, helped by E. Fry, 177
  Visit women prisoners in Newgate, 179
  Associations of, increase in number and scope, 182
  Lack of, in New South Wales, *183
  Convicts, often deported to New South Wales, *183
  Convicts, cared for during deportation, 184
  Fallen, 237
Women's Meetings had special care of unemployed maidservants, 74
  Often paid for education of poor children, 104
Wood, James, admonishes against handing spirituous liquors to others, 136(*)
Wool in antislavery agitation, 227
Wool spinning becomes a secondary occupation among country people, 53
Woolman, John, 13
  Interest in slavery, 206(*), 207(*)
  Journal, 207(*), *215
"Worldly arts" to be avoided, 101, 103
Worldly diversions, to be avoided, 31
Workhouses established because of number of unemployed,*54
  Developed from plans of J. Bellers, 75
  Called "poorhouses" after repeal of workhouse test,*91
Workhouse test repealed, 91

GENERAL INDEX

Working conditions, improvement of, 239

Works, good, with prayer, effect justification, 31

Wray, Sir Cecil, *211

Writing to be taught in Quaker school, 101

Parents in Penna. required to teach to their children, 109

Y

Yearly Meeting of New York, 135
Of Philadelphia, 135, 207
Of New England, 215
Of London: see **London Yearly Meeting**
The ultimate authority, 40
Origin of, 59
Public collections at, 61
Functions of, 61
At London, established 1660, *61

Yearly Meeting, names committee to consider education, 105
Attempts to see that all children attended school, 111
Appoints a committee to report on temperance question, 140
Advises total abstinence in 1835, 140

York, 158, 160, 223, *224
Location of Quaker insane asylum, The Retreat, 154, 155(*)
Duke of, 45, 200

York Retreat: see **Retreat**

York Trust Property Books, *116

Yorkshire, *116, *117
Quakers of, converted other Quakers to belief in total abstinence, 141
Quarterly Meeting of, 113, 155

Z

Zanzibar, freeing of Negroes in, 233